MY HORSE, MY SELF

LIFE LESSONS FROM TAOS HORSEWOMEN

MY HORSE, MY SELF

LIFE LESSONS FROM TAOS HORSEWOMEN

Susan Erlandson Washburn

Photographs by Jett Ulaner Sarachek

Library of Congress Cataloging-in-Publication Data

Washburn, Susan.
 My horse, my self : life lessons from Taos horsewomen / Susan Erlandson Washburn ; photographs by Jett Ulaner Sarachek.
 pages cm
 ISBN 978-1-937240-40-0 (pbk.) -- ISBN 978-1-937240-42-4 (ebook) 1. Horses--New Mexico--Taos--Anecdotes. 2. Women horse owners--New Mexico--Taos--Anecdotes. 3. Horsemen and horsewomen--New Mexico--Taos--Anecdotes. 4. Human-animal relationships--New Mexico--Taos--Anecdotes. I. Title.

SF301.W29 2014
636.1008997'496--dc23

2014009558

20141015
Casa de Snapdragon LLC
12901 Bryce Avenue, NE
Albuquerque, NM 87112
http://www.casadesnapdragon.com
Printed in the United States of America

CONTENTS

FOREWORD

THE HORSEWOMEN OF TAOS

"Riding a horse is not a gentle hobby, to be picked up and laid down like a game of solitaire. It is a grand passion. It seizes a person whole and, once it has done so, he will have to accept that his life will be radically changed."
— Ralph Waldo Emerson.

The women you will meet in this book have all been seized by this grand passion and transformed, often in profound and unexpected ways, by their equine relationships. They have been sustained in times of trouble; they have been healed from trauma; they have discovered strengths—and weaknesses—they didn't know they had. More importantly, they have experienced a deep and wordless connection with non-human sentient beings and through that, with the whole of creation. Their lives have indeed been radically changed; they have become more of who they really are because of their horses.

The particular women I chose to interview are not a representative sample of all the exceptional horsewomen in Taos. I shamelessly exploited my friends and friends of friends, choosing individuals I thought might have something unique or insightful to say about the intricate and intimate relationships we develop with the horses we love.

However, a funny thing happened when I took out my little digital recorder and asked my standard opening question, "How did you get involved with horses?" I kept getting the same answer: "I was born with the horse gene," or "I was a horse-crazy little girl," followed by a description of an intense interest in all things equine that surfaced in early childhood. Sometimes this occurred subsequent to experiences with real live horses, sometimes following merely literary and cinematic encounters, sometimes for no reason whatsoever. Then, after that initial confession of obsession, my interviewees told me amazing stories: of unconventional childhoods, romantic entanglements, marriages and divorces, births and deaths, health challenges, life-altering career changes. And all of these dramatic life events involved, either centrally or peripherally, horses.

Early-girlhood horse craziness was a common denominator in the stories, but it wasn't the only one. A second recurrent theme was the peculiarity of the ways in which these women got to Taos. Some moved here for conventional reasons, such as jobs or family connections; but far more ended up in Taos as a result of improbable synchronicities, compelling visions, or happy accidents. I was reminded of the notorious broken wagon wheel that stranded two New York painters here in 1898 and led to the founding of the Taos Society of Artists and the subsequent transformation of this remote village into a world-famous art colony.

Of course, local lore has it that only those summoned by Taos Mountain, the imposing peak that rises from the Sangre de Cristo range behind Taos Pueblo, will find it possible to settle here. When I was looking for property to buy in 2002, my realtor told me, quite seriously, "If the Mountain wants you, all doors will open. If it doesn't, nothing will work out and you'll leave." Presumably, the Mountain wanted these women.

Another local saying is "Taos is not for everybody," often quoted when the conversation involves someone who has just moved to more civilized environs, say Santa Fe or Boulder. In truth, Taos is not a place for the faint of heart. It retains characteristics of the frontier outpost it was less than a century ago, when justice was quick, personal and violent, and deals went down in smoke-filled backrooms. It was known then for its tough mountain men, Kit Carson being a prime example, and stalwart women.

The latter tradition, at least, has endured. Always a haven for renegade artists and literati, Taos attracted remarkably independent and unconventional ladies: Mabel Dodge Luhan, Dorothy Brett, Georgia O'Keefe, Millicent Rogers, and Agnes Martin, to name a few historical figures. Today a disproportionate number of women artists, writers, musicians, and entrepreneurs keep the local galleries, restaurants, and shops alive.

The horsewomen I interviewed are of this same hardy breed. The equestriennes I knew back East rode in raked arenas and boarded their horses in well-staffed stables. I like to think the ones I've met in Taos are a little gutsier, a little more down and dirty, a little more apt to change the flat tire on their horse trailers without calling AAA.

But why wouldn't they be? Living in Taos is challenging. This is a place of extremes, set in the starkly beautiful but inhospitable high desert, backed by rugged, nearly impassable mountains, topped with an expanse of sky so intensely blue it challenges the eye, a place where the days end in orange-vermillion sunsets so vivid they seem to belong on another planet. The weather is equally extreme, cycling from crop-killing droughts to blinding winter snowstorms, from pleasantly arid summer mornings to afternoon monsoons that darken the skies and hurl torrential rains and killer lightning bolts earthward.

Taos is also a place of social extremes. Three cultures coexist here, colorfully and sometimes uncomfortably. Tiwa-speaking Native Americans have inhabited beautiful Taos Pueblo, now an official World Heritage Site, for over a thousand years. The first Hispanics arrived in the sixteenth century with the Conquistadors, while Anglos didn't trickle in until the early 1800s. The mixture of customs and languages is rich but seasoned with resentment born of disparities in income and lifestyle. Drive down one of the county's potholed dirt roads and you'll see million-dollar pueblo-revival-style homes next to doublewides surrounded by junked automobiles. Stroll around the center of town and you'll find plenty of shops selling exquisite arts and crafts and artisan clothing. But for basic necessities you'll have to patronize Walmart, where you'll hear the lilting mix of Spanish and English distinctive to Northern New Mexico and discover that ordinary sales transactions involve inquiries about *la familia* and *su casa*.

And then there's the lack of anonymity. Taos is a small town where everybody knows your name and more about your personal affairs than your own mother. Living here is like belonging to a large, gossipy, extended family. This can be annoying when one is bent on committing some form of social indiscretion, but for a woman dealing with the vagaries of weather and hay suppliers, colics and injuries, and all the inevitable problems associated with owning horses, it's a good thing. Because Taos has minimal infrastructure, with only one resident equine vet and the nearest equine hospital a two-hour drive away, the horse people in town have to be both self-reliant and cooperative.

Most of the women I interviewed know one another. All of them would, I am confident, be prepared to help any one of the others in an emergency. For just as remarkable as these women are individually, they are more so collectively. There is a true community of horsewomen (and a few brave men) in Taos, and I am proud and grateful to be a part of it. The stories in this book are testimony to our common goal of striving to better our horses and our selves.

Cowgirls

Jennifer Romero

Pamela Bishop

Kimberly Swengel-Casara

Pam MacArthur

COWGIRLS

"A cowgirl is a woman with guts and a horse."
— Anonymous

JENNIFER ROMERO

"If I hadn't learned patience I wouldn't have gotten through to this horse."

I'm standing outside Jen Romero's neatly landscaped manufactured home. I'm leaning on a pipe corral that encloses a little green barn and its occupant, a pretty sorrel mare. Jen joins me and we watch the mare sort through a pile of hay for the tasty seed heads. We're talking quietly, tranquilized by the meditative calm that emanates from a grazing horse. If we look up, we can see the great rounded contours of Taos Mountain rising from the Pueblo lands to the north. The summit is obscured by drifts and wisps of morning clouds like a misty scene from a Japanese brush painting. With the parching heat of summer behind us, Taos seems a bit misty, its crisp clear air tempered by the humidity lingering from last night's rain.

I feel a wave of gratitude for whatever brought me to a place where it's still possible to have a horse in your backyard. Not to mention poultry. On the far side of Jen's house a flock of lushly feathered black chickens, safe in a tidy coyote-proof pen, are nibbling their own breakfasts. Next to them a flourishing vegetable garden overflows with leafy chard and corn and squash, promising an abundant harvest. I resolve to fertilize my straggly tomato plants and water them daily. Jen and her family are miles ahead of me on the road to agrarian self-sufficiency.

That shouldn't be surprising. Jen Romero is a pragmatic, hard-working woman with a youthful energy that far surpasses my own middle-aged need-a-nap-in-the-afternoon variety. She juggles her roles as wife, mother of two teenagers, and head of the medical billing department in a doctor's office efficiently and without drama.

But when it comes to the little mare eating breakfast in the paddock behind us, Jen is an unabashed romantic. Telling me how she came to buy Sassy Poco Lena, her voice takes on a lilt and her eyes sparkle; she sounds like a newly engaged woman describing meeting The One.

"I found a horse for sale here in Taos. It belonged to the local brand inspector and he did a little interview with me because he really liked this horse and wanted it to go to a good home. He'd bought it for his girlfriend, but she wasn't much of a rider. So I went over to his place and he had her in the round pen, all saddled. She just had this look about her; this glow seemed to be coming from her. I was in love with her the moment I saw her. There wasn't any question about whether it was the right horse for me; I was going to buy her regardless. I just felt this connection between us."

Sassy leaves her breakfast and ambles over to check me out. I've just come from feeding and grooming my own horse and my hands, which get thoroughly sniffed, carry the scent of my gelding. He would be pleased with her interest; he fancies himself quite the ladies' man.

"She's a sweet, friendly girl," Jennifer says fondly, reaching over the fence to stroke Sassy's neck. "I could see that about her right away."

Actually, Jen's impetuous decision to purchase Sassy even though she had never before owned a horse wasn't as rash as it might appear. As a horse-crazy little girl she had the perfect grandparents: they owned a ranch in southern Utah and kept horses. Needless to say, this pretty much guaranteed extensive summer visits from their granddaughter.

Back home, on the outskirts of Salt Lake City, Jen found another way to fulfill her passion for horses. She found a pair in a field near her home and, unbeknownst to her parents, regularly sneaked away to ride them bareback. When she tells me this I confess that I had done the same thing as a nine year old growing up on the outskirts of Tuscaloosa, Alabama. My desire to be with, and preferably on, a horse, any horse, was as strong and lawless as a full-blown addiction. I know exactly how Jen must have felt, how she must have plotted her secret forays to the neighbor's pasture, her stomach fluttering with butterflies of anticipation.

However, as with many of us who have ridden early in life and then endured years of horse-deprivation, college, career, and child-rearing soon took precedence over equine pleasures. As a young woman and adult, Jen had little contact with horses until she moved to Taos with her husband and teenage children. But she did have a plan: she made sure the residential property they purchased was horse-friendly and she bought a horse trailer even though she had nothing to put in it. The stage was set for that fated meeting with Sassy.

But, Jen admits, she knew nothing about taking care of a horse, and, as it turned out, she didn't know that much about the beautiful "glowing" mare she had fallen in love with.

"When I went back to pick Sassy up, I think she was sad to leave her friends and a little scared because she hollered at her previous owner when she got in the trailer and we drove away. I had some help when I unloaded her at Pam MacArthur's boarding stable, but it was nearly dark and I didn't want to leave her. I really wanted to have a little sleepover inside her corral.

"She seemed comfortable with me and I wasn't scared that she would hurt me in any way, so the next day I just saddled her up and took off down the road. I didn't even ride her in the arena. I was used to riding out and I'd never had a horse misbehave with me. She was fine even though halfway home a bunch of dogs ran out behind us. I guess she felt I was her leader.

"We had several good experiences like this and then, after a week, things suddenly changed. I got on her in the arena and she threw me off. It was deliberate. It was 'Get off my back I'm testing you now.' This was just shocking to me. I really didn't know what to do so I crawled over to her and I got back on because I was so scared that if I didn't then I never would. So I rode her a bit and then put her back in her stall.

"It took me quite some time to get over that and she knew it. Each time I took her out she would do something to challenge me. Everything I had imagined about having a horse was completely thrown away because I'd never experienced a horse acting that way. I took it personally. I cried. I felt like she hated me. I thought about selling her, because maybe I wasn't the right person for her. That was truly devastating because I had really fallen in love with her."

Jen had to drop her expectations and get to know the horse she actually had as opposed to the horse she thought she had. What she found out was quite interesting: the horse she felt such an instant attraction to happened to be the equine equivalent of herself.

"After probing everyone I could about their experiences I found out that it's a reality that you get thrown sometimes. Pam Bishop helped me get through that rough spot. Without having someone knowledgeable supporting me I don't know that I would have gotten through it on my own.

"I've come to know Sassy much better now. We have very similar personalities. I've thought about this a lot. She's very sensitive to everything and she learns quickly. I'm that way too. I pick up things fast. When we're out riding with other horses, Sassy's definitely a leader. She wants to be in front and she hollers at the other horses if she can't see them. She's a kind of take-charge girl, like me. She's challenging in that she'll do what I ask, but she doesn't always do it with a willing attitude. She's a little stubborn, and we connect in that way too."

Seeing the similarities between oneself and one's horse can sometimes be a shock if the character traits reflected back to us are ones we habitually deny. Jennifer, however, saw parts of herself that she was well aware of, parts that have served her well in her career and her family life. But she still had something to learn from Sassy, her take-charge kind of mare.

"I've had to learn a lot of patience in dealing with her. If I hadn't learned patience I wouldn't have gotten through to this horse. It made a huge difference. It's interesting how the dynamics of our relationship have helped me in dealing with people at work. I see herd dynamics in my everyday life. There's a leader, a protector, and there are followers. With Sassy I used patience and repetition and I expected her to do things right; and if she didn't, I gave a little nudge until she did. And I've learned to do that in my work environment. I expect people to do the right thing, and if they don't, I give them a little nudge in the right direction. With Sassy I give a lot of praise and I've incorporated the same thing into my work. My co-workers all learn differently just like horses do. Some get it right away, some take longer. I've even used these same tactics–patience, repetition, and praise–with my two children and they really do work."

Jen goes on to talk about the way in which Sassy has forced her to become more in touch with her feelings or suffer the consequences.

"After I got thrown off I thought about it and I felt like maybe I'd been so nervous that day that she couldn't take it anymore and she just had to get rid of me. So I tried grounding myself. I'd have to do deep breathing while I was sitting on her before we rode off because I could feel myself getting scared and nervous and I could feel her tightening up under me. It's interesting how you pick up on each other like that; it's like you just become one.

"So now being with her makes me notice if I'm in a negative mood, because she will react to it. If I get a reaction from her I take a step back and ask myself if it's something about me or is it just her. I've also noticed that when I'm feeling bummed out and I'm really aware of it she will generally be more drawn to me. She'll just stand there and let me love on her and that brings me peace. But if I go out there and I've got all this energy and my brain is going ninety miles an hour, she tends to keep her distance. All that energy is just too much for her."

As we are winding up the interview session, Jen smiles as she contemplates her serendipitous meeting with Sassy.

"Think about it," she says. "I'm looking for a horse. There happens to be a horse right here in Taos, a young Quarter Horse, just what I wanted. I walk over there and fall in love with this horse who is exactly the horse I was looking for. How does that happen? It's like it was…" she pauses, shaking her head in disbelief, "…like it was meant to be."

PAMELA BISHOP

"I've learned a lot from the big-name guys, but I don't buy into the idea that each of them has the one and only way to train horses."

The dirt road winding through the sagebrush to the house Pam Bishop shares with her partner, Keith Randall, and their baby daughter Kara, seems to be heading in the wrong direction. I'm wondering if I missed a turn somewhere. But as I head up an incline a large barn comes into view. It's not the usual metal outbuilding common in these parts, but a handsome wood-sided structure. Now I know I'm on the right track; Keith's family owns a lumberyard in Taos.

Still, I'm not prepared for the house I see after rounding another curve. It's built of logs, seriously massive logs, with a pitched roof, a grand pillared portal, and floor to ceiling windows framing a view of the eastern foothills, the sprawl of greater Taos, such as it is, and major mountains to the north. This is not your typical New Mexican flat-roofed, stucco-walled pueblo revival dwelling. It's more akin to the upscale wanna-be-a-cowboy ranch houses that you find in Jackson Hole. It's also the kind of house I've always wanted for myself and I'm having a serious attack of casa envy.

Pam greets me at the front door, intercepting a menacing-looking pit bull mix that's come out to either greet me or eat me. Pam reassures me that the dog is friendly and Kara, who's perched on her right hip, gives me a high five and a big smile. She's confident and outgoing at nine months of age. I make a mental note to ask Pam if her child-rearing practices have been derived from her horse-training techniques; Pam's horses are famously well mannered.

As we perch on high stools at a rustic granite bar in the great room, Kara playing at our feet, Pam tells me how she got to where she is now. Like the road to her house, her personal path has had a few bumps and twists. But from the outset, it's been marked by hoof prints.

"Horses have always been part of my life. My great grandfather on my dad's side trained horses for the U.S. Cavalry in Kansas. My dad worked for the Forest Service and we lived in New Mexico and Arizona, but wherever we were we always had horses. My first horse, when I was about six, was a little Shetland pony named Sugar who was anything but sweet, but we loved her anyway. All three of us kids would ride triple on her. Our next horse was a little Arab named Juan. He took care of us and taught us to ride. When I went to school I couldn't wait to get home to see him. Once I was grounded from riding for doing something to my sister, but I snuck down to the barn and got Juan and rode him bareback in the pipe corral until I fell off and hit my head. I went up to the house and told my mother that nothing had happened, but she made me lie down and wait for my father to come home. I was terrified that I would be in big trouble, but he just sat down on the edge of my bed and said, 'Baby, if you're going to ride, at least use a halter.'

When Pam went off to New Mexico State University in Las Cruces, she didn't really know what she was doing. Her grades the first two years were, in her words, "terrible." However, her love of horses got her back on track. She signed up for a class in beginning western horsemanship, a prerequisite for the courses in equine studies that she wanted to take.

"I'd ridden all my life and had just finished competing for state fair queen so when the instructor saw me ride and she told me I didn't belong in this class I thought she was kicking me out because I was riding improperly. I'd never had lessons; I just rode instinctively. I was surprised when she told me to come back and join her advanced students. Then she told me I didn't belong in that class either, but she wanted me in her program and asked me to help the students who had fear issues. This was my first experience with teaching and I loved it.

"I did that in the mornings and in the afternoons I rode donated horses to evaluate their suitability as lesson horses. I was riding all sorts of different horses and loving it and a side effect was that my grades came up from a 2.5 to a 3.9 because of having a focus."

This experience took Pam a few significant miles down the road to where she is now. But she still had a lot to learn, and one of the things she learned early on was to drop her assumptions about what a horse should know and do and to recognize and work with whatever was standing on four legs in front of her.

"During my senior year I started my first horse in a class taught by an instructor whom I'd shown under when he was a judge. I had a tough little horse and I'd never done any of this round penning and sacking out and driving stuff. We'd always had broke horses at home. I was so terrified of disappointing my teacher that I actually had panic attacks.

"So I took a few days off from anything horse-related during vacation and came back with a new sense of purpose. I forgave my little horse for not knowing anything. I had expected her to know all this stuff and she just didn't. Once I came at it with a different mindset and adopted her point of view, she was a gem. She did everything I asked her to do, walk, trot, lope.

"At the same time I was working with a big Quarter Horse mare just off the track. She was a sweet easy horse, but she wouldn't lope on the left lead. So I was struggling with this unbroke horse and this big mare and I was sitting in an economics class thinking about both of them and suddenly a light bulb went off in my head: that mare has never been *taught* to pick up a left lead. I ditched my next class and went down to the barn and taught the mare what to do. I finally realized I needed to step up and teach these horses rather than assume that they knew things. This totally changed the way I approached horses. Around the same time I was introduced to natural horsemanship, which I hadn't known anything about. I used what I learned from it on my barrel racing horse who was all go and no whoa and couldn't do anything but run barrels. Within a week I was able to ride him without a bridle."

After graduation Pam moved to Denver and horses got put on hold while she concentrated on making a living. She had majored in finance at her mother's insistence that she study something practical, but she wasn't happy about it. Had it not been for the maternal nudging to acquire some marketable skills, Pam says she would have stayed in Las Cruces and worked for one of her equine studies professors as a rider.

"I regret that I wasn't able to stand up for myself and say, yes, this is what I want to do. Because I think where would I be now if I had done something I really had a passion for, something horse-related? Would I have had the same struggles I've had in my business as a real estate appraiser? In my fantasy world I just train horses and give clinics, but I know it's not smart to rely on the horse world as a sole source of income because it's too risky."

Sometimes mother does know best.

However, Pam's road to the horse was only blocked temporarily. In 1992 she moved back to Taos, got married and began working as a real estate appraiser. By 2002 her business was generating enough income to support a horse so she went shopping. She intended to buy a horse to ride, but somehow she ended up with two weanling fillies from foundation Quarter Horse bloodlines similar to those of the little mare she had trained in her college days.

"A woman I happened to meet at a conference sent me a video of a filly she'd picked up at an Oregon dispersal sale. She thought I'd like her because she had strong King breeding. So I watch the video and just fall in love with this filly, who's a weanling. What on earth am I going to do with a weanling? But the price was right so I drove to Phoenix to get her. My husband at the time, who knows nothing about horses, is wandering around the barn and spots this other bay filly and asks if I've seen her. He suggests that I take both fillies and then sell the one I don't want. And of course the second one is a weanling too. So I end up with two babies, Annie, the foundation stock mare, and Jackie, who is more refined and showy. They've just turned seven and I still have both of them.

"These horses have given me such great opportunities. I started them when they were two and I gained confidence that I actually knew what I was doing. Even then I never thought I could train other people's horses. But when I began riding with other people they commented on how well behaved my horses were and asked me if I could do with their horses whatever I had done with mine."

What Pam did with her horses evolved over time as she came to trust her own instincts and move towards a kinder, gentler approach to working with her horses.

"I did a one-week clinic with a big name trainer and it turned my world around. I wanted to become a certified trainer using his methods so I started the certification program, but found out in three weeks that big name certification is all about the money. I didn't finish the program. I've learned a lot from the big name guys, but I don't buy into the idea that each of them has the one and only way to train horses.

"I started Reddy Freddy, my little unbroke project horse, using a different technique than what I used with Annie and Jackie. I bought Reddy on impulse at an auction in Belen. She was in with a bunch of horses and she looked at me and I looked at her and that was it. It was kismet. She was not correct; she was two and a half and thirteen hands and maybe five hundred pounds. Her feet were like pancakes and she had swollen places on her butt and her knees and she wasn't even halter broke. But there was something about her…"

Whatever that something was, it touched Pam in a deeper place than her previous horses had and perhaps because of the emotional resonance with this particular horse, Pam altered her training techniques.

"When I worked with her I never hurt her or scared her. I expected less and rewarded more. I didn't have marathon sessions with her. If she let me put the halter on her and apply a little bit of pressure on the lead rope and she simply looked at me that was great. We were done. If she let me brush her just a little that was enough. I broke things down into tiny steps. And within a week she was halter broke and would stand for the farrier and the vet."

Breaking, if one can use that term, a horse in this way creates a far more trusting and intimate horse-human relationship than more authoritarian techniques. Keeping an eye on Kara, who's emptying the contents of my purse on the floor, Pam relates the following story.

"Reddy's kind and trusting. She just goes with the flow. I'm not confrontational and she's not confrontational. When I was pregnant with Kara, Reddy was the last horse I rode before I stopped riding completely. Then the most amazing thing happened in December when I was nearly seven months pregnant. It was snowing and I couldn't open the paddock gate to feed the horses because of a snowdrift, so I would back the trailer to the fence, climb onto it, and fork over the hay in three different spots. I had fed the other girls and I was putting the last pile out for Reddy when she started to leave. I was tired and not feeling well, so I said, 'Well at least one of you could come over and help me down off this fence.' And that little horse came back and lined herself up with the fence so I could lean on her to get down. I was shocked. After that whenever I was down with the horses Reddy stayed with me and put herself between the other horses and me. When Kara would shift inside me from one side to the other Reddy would move to protect whichever side she was on. It was fascinating, like a science experiment. I love that little horse. I love my other girls too, but Reddy Freddy will never be sold. Never."

At this point Kara has to be restrained from eating the coins she's extracted from my purse and I remember to ask Pam about her ideas on child rearing.

"I never thought I'd be a mom, but now I am and the horse training stuff carries over. I'm trying to follow the model I used for Reddy. I can't put Kara in a round pen to let her run around and scrub off her excess energy, but when she's older I can have her sweep the floor, or muck out a horse pen or wash a car. I want her to be confident and not be limited by being a girl. I want her to know what all the knives and forks are for and to be able to sit at a table with the President of the United States if the occasion arises. I also want her to be able to walk into a garage and say, 'I need my car fixed and this is what's wrong with it.' I don't want her to be a bitch, but I want her to be assertive and also to appreciate everyone for whatever they have to offer. I'm going to teach her this in small steps using lots of praise. If she takes everything out of a drawer and puts just one item back, that's fabulous."

With some encouragement, Kara replaces my wallet in my purse and we both thank her and tell her how incredibly clever she is. No round pen needed.

KIMBERLY SWENGEL-CASARA

"I learned to sense when I had this zingy energy and bring myself down by breathing really deep and focus on grounding it through my feet."

Last year Kimberly Swengel-Casara posted a striking photo of herself on Facebook. She's wearing a big black cowboy hat and a triumphant smile and she's at the controls of a huge roller compactor. A swath of bare dirt has been cut through the sagebrush in front of her. The caption reads, "Just built my first road!"

That photo pretty much sums up the last five years of Kimberly's thirteen-year residence in Taos. Pam Bishop's road to the horse-centric life she now enjoys took a few unexpected turns, but the map was drawn from her childhood experiences. In contrast, Kimberly rerouted her life in her mid-forties. She transformed herself from a businesswoman whose previous careers included buyer for a Beverly Hills shoe store and proprietor of an Italian restaurant into a contemporary cowgirl who rounds up cattle for friends and owns a small horse-boarding facility. This transformation, which I've witnessed firsthand, has been entirely self-initiated. Kimberly did not come from a ranching family nor did she have much experience with horses. What she did have was a powerful vision and the determination to manifest it.

"I always wanted a horse and I rode a bit when I was around thirteen, but I got my arm broken when I was thrown, and my parents wouldn't let me ride any more. Then on my forty-first birthday, my stepfather, John Farnsworth, who is well-known for his paintings of horses, said to me, 'This is not a dress rehearsal. This is your life and you better start living it because all you do is work.' Which was true. I had been working about seventy hours a week at our restaurant. All I did was work and sleep and take care of my two boys.

"My stepfather's statement made me reflect about getting some happiness in my life instead of all this stress. I turned forty-one on the last day of April and by September of that year I had my first horse. I didn't know anything about horses. I paid way too much for him and he was lame and no good for riding. He fell down several times while I was on him. So I kept him for three years and loved on him and then I bought Tilly, a fifteen-year-old Paso Fino who is now about twenty-one.

"Tilly was a really good teacher for me. People who have ridden her call her 'Tilly the Wonder Horse.' She's a real schoolmistress. She taught me a lot about being a horsewoman, more than just about how to hold my hands or sit my seat."

Perhaps the most important thing Tilly taught Kimberly was the necessity of monitoring her inner state. Much like Jen Romero, Kimberly had a horse who was highly sensitive to her emotional energy.

"Tilly would run away from me when I first had her. She got as far away from me in the field as she could. And that made me feel bad because I wanted her to want to be with me. But I was just through the roof with my energy and at the time I had no ability to recognize it or to realize that I was way overly energetic compared to most people. Tilly's energy was also through the roof. She's an absolute mirror of me.

"So I learned to sense when I had this zingy energy going and bring myself down by breathing really deep and focus on grounding every bit of that energy that was spraying out of me and direct it down through my feet and into the earth. It was a mental exercise and I had to work at it.

Even so, I had another horse tell me about it last year. I was a way more experienced horsewoman than when I got Tilly six years ago and I thought I was really cool. But when I went out to present myself to this little red Arab who belonged to a friend she gave me a look with her pretty little face and immediately these words came into my mind: 'Wow, you are way too prickly for me, lady.' That horse told me clearly in about five seconds that my energy was too 'prickly' for her and she moved away from me with this nasty look on her face like, 'no way lady are you getting near me.' I had to do that same exercise, the big breath, the big emotional cleansing, and drop the energy down into the ground through my feet. As soon as I did that the horse walked right up to me. It was a revelation to me on two levels: one, that I could control my emotions and energy, and two, that horses really do communicate telepathically. There's not a doubt in my mind about that now. The word 'prickly' was the key. It wasn't a word I would ever have used unless I was describing a prickly pear cactus."

Now, at age forty-seven, Kimberly cares for several boarded horses in addition to her own two, teaches riding, and trains horses. She's come a long way from the woman who was so frightened of the lame palomino she had just bought that she would throw his hay over the fence rather than enter his paddock to feed him. And who "nearly had a heart attack when my instructor told me to pick up his hoof and clean it."

"There's a complete correlation between the horses I've had and the way I've evolved as a horsewoman and as a person. I learned my seat and hands and how to control myself on Tilly because at first she was so fast she would run circles around everyone on trail rides. Then I got more confident and she calmed down and now she's a school horse and I'm a riding instructor. The confidence I got from learning to handle Tilly enabled me to take on training Ringo, whom I got when he was two."

Ringo, a handsome sixteen hand black gaited gelding, is Kimberly's principal mount and, as she puts it, her "number one son."

Ironically enough, she bought him as an afterthought on a shopping trip to find a mature horse for one of her boys.

"We went to this barn in Texas that specialized in spotted saddle horses. So there was this solid black Tennessee Walking Horse off separately and they weren't showing him to anybody. But every time I walked by his stall he'd look out and give me that big soft eye. Finally I asked the guy who was bringing out the horses, 'Why aren't you showing me this little fellow?' And the man says, 'Oh, you don't want him. He ain't got no spots. And he's just a two year old. You definitely don't want him.'

I wanted to see how he moved, so the man brought him out, but asked the trainer to ride him. At the time that didn't mean much to me, but in hindsight I realize it was because the horse wasn't broke. Later I found out he'd only been under saddle three times. If I'd known that I'd never have bought him. But in my ignorance I got on him and, of the eleven horses I'd ridden that day, he was the best. His whole attitude was accommodating, no head throwing, no resistance, and his gait was so smooth and he was so beautiful. My trainer agreed he was the best of all the horses we'd seen.

"Now Ringo's six and he's like this little ball of clay that I molded to be my horse. I've had several horses and, like my children, I love them all immensely. But Ringo's the one I'm most bonded to and he's the most bonded to me. He gets his nose out of joint when I ride the other horses. He looks at me like he's saying, 'You don't love me anymore.' None of my other horses give me that look, just Ringo.

"He still has his little boy moments. He's energetic and a little willful, but he has more control of his energy, which is a reflection of how I've changed from when I got Tilly. I'm still energetic, but I'm way more grounded. I still like to compete and do well and win and Ringo's always ready to lope and compete. He's a reflection of me, of course, but he's not hyper and now I'm not either."

Far from it. Kimberly's work with horses forced her to calm down and find herself and this in turn gave her the confidence to launch a new career as an equine professional. A staunch political conservative, she's a living example of entrepreneurial spirit combined with down-home pragmatism; she built most of her boarding facility herself with the aid of her big blue tractor and a little hired help. Kimberly sums up the result of her four years of hard work as she points at the horses in the tidy paddocks adjoining her riding arena.

"Look at all this. Can you believe it? I'm living my dream."

PAM MAC ARTHUR

"Every horse doesn't have to be perfect; they just have to be right for what you need them to do."

It's mid-September, the sweetest time of the year in Taos. The leaves of the lofty cottonwoods lining El Tros Road are still green, but their chartreuse streaks tell me they're thinking about changing color. In a week or so the willows and elms along the acequias will take on a yellow glow in the sunlight and the aspens will splash patches of amber among the dark evergreens blanketing the sides of Taos Mountain. Another New Mexican summer is about to end in an explosion of gold.

I squeeze my SUV past a particularly burly cottonwood trunk and park beside a row of pipe corrals. A sign, "MacArthur Quarter Horses," assures me that I'm in the right place and as I walk down a dirt path between the corrals several Quarter Horses assure me that they wouldn't say no to an early dinner.

The path ends at a rustic adobe house and Pam MacArthur, accompanied by an effusively friendly border collie, comes out to meet me. She's wearing faded jeans and a well-used cowboy hat, the garb I usually see her in at Taos Saddle Club meetings, where the perfection of her manicure never fails to amaze me. I can't understand how a working horsewoman can maintain such long, beautiful fingernails. She must have the human equivalent of good hoof genes.

The front door opens into a cozy low-ceilinged living room that has the secure, en-closed feel of traditional pueblo revival interiors. The room is full of stuff, lots of stuff, all of it interesting. To the left of the entrance are shelves holding a collection of very old, very fragile Native American pottery. Some of the pots look like the rare specimens I've seen in Taos' Millicent Rogers Museum. In front of me two pairs of fancy fringed chaps and some silver-encrusted headstalls hang from hooks on the wall. On a table to the right is a display of enormous silver trophy belt buckles that you can bet were won in rodeos, not purchased from Ralph Lauren. Some of the furniture looks like inherited antiques, as does a beautiful pendulum clock ticking in a corner.

"As you can see we're collectors," Pam tells me. Well, yes. Pam and her husband Johnny have been married thirty-seven years and this room holds the physical evidence of their conjoined lives.

One life began in Vermont, where Johnny, who now fabricates artistic metal products, gates and signs and almost any kind of ironwork one might need for ranch or home, learned his first trade, clockmaking. He was apprenticed to a Scottish clockmaker and, Pam tells me, "He didn't just make the cases for clocks; he made the entire insides. He cut the gears from sheets of brass."

The other life, Pam's, began in Texas, where Pam's great, great grandfather and his two brothers settled three sections of land near Fort Worth and where Pam spent her childhood hanging out with horses and cows on the family dairy farm.

These two lives converged in Taos at the height of the hippie migration. Pam showed up in 1972 to study in the fine arts graduate program at Southern Methodist University's Fort Burgwin campus southeast of town. Johnny drove out from Vermont with his aunt to visit relatives and to make sure her aging Volkswagen didn't break down en route. Once here, he bought a garage and set up shop as a mechanic. When Pam came in with a malfunctioning Mercedes and no money for repairs, he fixed it anyway and that was the start of their long and happy relationship.

When Pam first came to Taos she, along with other SMU students and faculty, lived in the Mabel Dodge Luhan House. This historic dwelling was the former home of Mabel Dodge, ex-East Coast socialite and doyenne of the arts, and her Pueblo-born fourth husband, Tony Luhan. In Taos' early days as a swinging art colony it housed guests such as Georgia O'Keefe, D.H. Lawrence, and Martha Graham. Dennis Hopper purchased the house in 1970 and made sure it continued to be a venue for both artistic endeavors and serious partying.

Pam met Hopper when she worked at the Modern Art Museum in Fort Worth and the Museum hosted an exhibit of his photographs. Shortly after she moved to Taos he hired her to manage his little gallery on Kit Carson Road.

"We showed a lot of contemporary art there, Andy Warhol soup can paintings, Bruce Conner's cobweb-encrusted assemblages, the work of artists I knew from my Fort Worth days. We also had items from Dennis' own collection. He was an incredible collector, but working for him was kind of iffy and crazy. I was working for fifty dollars a week plus commission which wasn't enough to live on so I quit and worked as a silversmith. I had learned silversmithing from Rowena and Cinco Martinez, who had a trading post called El Rincon, just east of La Dona Luz Restaurant, where Dennis and his friends would while away the afternoons in the bar playing liars' poker.

"Meanwhile I had moved from the Mabel Dodge House to a lovely crumbling adobe managed by Carmen Velarde, the famous fireplace *enjarradora* [a builder of masonry kiva-style fireplaces]. It was next door to R.C. Gorman's place, and he would come out on his balcony and whistle at my boyfriends.

"Later, after Johnny and I got married, we left Taos for a while. We needed to get some cash together so we could buy a piece of land and build a house. We went down to the oil fields in southern New Mexico. This was in 1974 when oil was booming. We were there for two years, living in a converted school bus in the oil patch. It was definitely a mind-broadening time. We were not the usual sort of people you find in a place like that. But we saved enough money to buy this piece of land and build the first part of this house."

At this point I ask Pam when horses entered her life. It turns out they were there all along.

"When I was just a little tyke hanging out on the family's dairy farm they would send me out with a stick and tell me to bring the bulls in. You want to start kids around livestock early so they aren't afraid. Then they learn to take charge of a situation and how to move a cow by stepping one way or another to direct it.

"I had a pony as a child and a horse while I was in high school and then much later a little paint horse here in Taos. But I didn't get involved with cutting horses until sometime around 1986. I had bred a mare I owned to a very nice son of Doc Olena and I liked the people that owned him and I liked their stock and I wanted to learn the sport.

"I started competing seriously in 1987 and showed for two years, but cutting requires money and time and I wasn't able to do it again until the mid nineties. Then I showed nearly every year until 2004. I didn't win a lot of money over that time, maybe $8,000, but of course I wasn't doing it for the money. I loved it because it's a real team sport. There's not only you and the cow out in the pen, there are four people helping you; two herd holders on really tall horses who keep the herd together and help you select the cow you want to cut, and two turn-back riders on smaller horses who keep the cow in play by turning it back towards you. You just use whoever's around and then you help them when they're cutting. You develop such friendships with these people. That was the most rewarding thing. I know people all over Texas and New Mexico from showing. You visit and get to know the husbands and wives and kids and dogs and horses. You know where they live and you might stay at their ranch if you're passing through and need a place to put your horse overnight. It's a big family and it's unlike any other horse sport I know because it's so much more cooperative. There's a lot of camaraderie.

"Of course cutting makes you really learn to pay attention. You aren't assigned your cow; you pick it. You need to watch the cattle before you go in so you get a feel for which ones might behave well and which ones might be difficult. You don't want one that's shifty eyed or got its head too high or keeps stepping back into the herd. You want one that hasn't been exhausted by a previous competitor and one that doesn't dart away when a horse walks by. You want a cow with a low head and a soft expression. If you're riding in the open classes you might want one that looks a little more challenging so you can show what you can do. I personally liked to cut cows with a little bit of Brahma in them—they call it 'having ear' because the Brahma's have long ears—because these cows tend to be more active and hold up better in competition."

Pam's competitive days are now over; she sold her last cutting horse in 2004. But she still follows the sport, travelling to some shows and watching others on television or the web. Many of her contemporaries have also stopped actively participating; age brings limitations and cutting isn't exactly a pony ride in the park. However, the bonds that were formed during those high-tension moments in the arena remain.

"I was a little sad at first when I went to a show and I wasn't out there riding, but now I have just as good a time watching and being with my friends. A lot of them aren't competing either, but are still involved peripherally, either with breeding or through horses they've bought or sold."

Pam and Johnny tried breeding cutting horses for a time. However, they soon abandoned the venture in favor of providing a service that was desperately needed in Taos.

"Breeding's a disaster unless you're very well financed and have top bloodlines. It's always hard to sell what you breed. But we had this land and access to riding trails and I noticed that people were continually looking for a place to keep their horses since most people only want to own one horse. So I changed over to being primarily a boarding stable."

Pam has had many horses in her life. She mentions a few and I get the impression that they have been, quite appropriately, working partners, members of a team of two. I'm curious as to whether she was emotionally attached to any of them so I ask if she had ever felt a special connection with any of her horses. She answers promptly and decisively.

"That would be Divot, the mare I had to euthanize a few months ago. She was special. My cutting horses were more exciting and I won money and championships on them, but I'd use one for three or four years and then sell it and get a better horse. But I had Divot all along. I got her from Mrs. Troy at Casa de Caballos [a Taos boarding and training stable] where I had been working. I broke Divot for her son-in-law to ride, but at about age three she started bucking everyone off, myself included. The Troys were going to sell her to the killers so I asked Mrs. Troy to give her to me instead of a Christmas bonus.

"I had Divot for fifteen years. She was a gorgeous mare, beautifully gaited, and she was a total enigma. You never knew what horse she was going to be when you went out to the stables. She was a very quick learner and very athletic; she always had her four feet right under her and was always ready to respond. Within a few weeks of riding her I had her comfortably taking both leads from the halt.

"She was drop dead perfect in the arena. I could just breathe on her side and she would elevate into a perfect canter and spin for me. She would do anything I asked of her except pass by scary things on the trail. She was terrified of everything. I think before the Troys gave her to me she may have been abused by some of the workers at the stables. She was a true challenge. There was always a lot of negotiation with that horse and she taught me a lot of humility because I never knew what to expect of her.

"She talked to me, though. She always said hello when I went into the barn and when I walked by her stall, she called to me. But at one point I sold her because she bit people and I couldn't have that in my boarding stable. When I left her with the new owner and drove away she screamed. It was just tragic, so incredibly sad. I wept all the way home.

"The new owner kept her for a year and a half and during that time she foundered, so he decided to give her back to me. He delivered her one day while I was away. Johnny called me and I came home and saw her in a little pen with a bunch of people around her. She hadn't seen me in nearly two years and when I came driving up I called her name and her head went up and she neighed as if she were saying, 'Thank God you're back! Thank God *I'm* back!' Her recognition of me was so amazing I knew I had to take care of this horse forever.

"Of all the horses I had I learned the most from her. I consider myself patient, but she was very impatient. We were different in just about every way. It was like opposites attract. I had to spend a lot of time comforting her to keep her from being afraid of the world. I've always been able to quiet excited horses by just going and standing near them and using my calmness to help them. So Divot and I complemented each other. Also, I was a good rider and she needed to be ridden well.

"The main thing I learned from her was not to have expectations. I would go out and it might be one of the days that she was exceptionally fearful, so I would have to abandon what I planned to do and go back to the basics. You have no control over what your horse is like in the morning when you go out to the corral. You can have a grand prix horse or a raging bronc. The only thing you can do is make that horse be better at the end of the ride and yourself be a better horseperson. My friends all said Divot had some wires crossed and she probably did have some visual handicap or lack of connection between the two sides of her brain. I had to accept that.

"Divot absolutely did teach me humility and to be more tolerant of people. She made me slow down and think about what I say and do and the consequences of that. I've had a lot of great horses that I have felt very connected with who helped me achieve my goals of showing and finding out who I was, but I learned more from Divot than anyone. Making the decision to euthanize her was the most awful thing I've ever had to do. I was resigned to not riding her ever again because of her second round of founder and I was content just to keep her and talk to her. But this bout was so severe that the bone had completely detached from the hoof wall and was starting to bulge out through the sole. She was still the same horse; she was still happy to see me, but she only had three legs. I knew I just had to let her go."

Divot is gone, but hardly forgotten. A framed portrait of her has pride of place in the MacArthur's combination library and trophy room. And she left a legacy, a daughter,

Prima, who is now five years old. Prima is chestnut, a bit smaller than her mother, but with the same finely angled shoulders, white-blazed face and soft eyes. Like her mother, she has an aversion to the screaming peacocks, barking dogs and various sheep and cattle that live along El Tros road. However, Prima did not inherit her athletic mother's high energy or enthusiasm for work. Once again Pam was forced to realize the futility of having preconceived ideas about what a given horse can or can't do.

"It was unfair of me to expect Prima to be like Divot. Prima does have a nice fast walk, but she is who she is. I have to get over my expectations for her. After all, every horse doesn't have to be perfect; they just have to be right for what you need them to do."

What Pam needed a horse to do was to ride out in the mountains with companions. Rather than trying to cope with Prima's possible misbehavior on the trail, she bought a second horse, the aptly named Dulcie, a quiet well-bred mare of illustrious Quarter Horse parentage.

"Having Dulcie, whom I can count on to be good on the trail, takes the pressure off Prima. I can let her be who she is and work with that."

Which is the best thing we can do with the horses—and the people—in our lives.

Mothers, Daughters, and Horses

Kim Ann Treiber-Thompson

Susan Nestor

Christine Morehart

Jennifer Siegel

MOTHERS, DAUGHTERS, AND HORSES

*"He has galloped through a young girl's dreams,
added richness to grown women's lives..."*
—Toni Robinson

KIM ANN TREIBER-THOMPSON

"I just want a horse friend again."

I f you stop at the Adobe Bar in the historic Taos Inn on the right night you can enjoy one of their famous Cowboy Buddha Margaritas to the accompaniment of foot-tapping, twangy country music. At the back of the roofed-over courtyard, silhouetted against an adobe wall, you'll see a slender woman with a cascade of wavy blonde hair fronting four instrumentalists. Her sweetly resonant voice soars over the usual crowd of local eccentrics and camera-toting tourists. Lucky you! Kim and the Caballeros are performing and I guarantee that, whatever your mood when you entered the bar, it will be better when you leave, especially if the group performs "On My Pony," Kim's tribute to the trail-riding ladies of Taos.

Kim Ann Treiber-Thompson (her husband, Chipper Thompson, is an instrumentalist in the band as well as a songwriter) didn't set out to be a country western singer. Trained in psychology and counseling, her musical tastes ran to folk-rock, possibly in reaction to the classic country music that her mother had played incessantly when Kim was growing up. But eventually the maternal imprinting took effect and in 2003 Kim put together the Caballeros.

That maternal imprinting wasn't restricted to music; it was also the source of Kim's lifelong love of horses.

"My mother was a closet cowgirl. When I was six years old she took me to the Chicago Amphitheater to see Roy Rogers and Dale Evans. The lights went on and the music came up and in came Roy Rogers on Trigger. I thought I would pee my pants. The whole regalia, the mane, the tail…I could care less about Roy. It was all about Trigger."

When Kim was in third grade her mother enrolled both of them in English riding lessons at a stable near their home in northern Illinois and their shared interest in all things equine grew, until Kim's mother became pregnant and the riding lessons went by the wayside. However, another pivotal experience was on the way. The family took a road trip out west that included a week at the Bishops Lodge outside Santa Fe. At that time, guests were assigned a personal horse to ride and groom for the duration of their stay.

"I was about nine years old and I was completely hooked," Kim says. "I can still remember my horse's name, Mescalero. We rode every day up in the mountains above Santa Fe and at the end of the week they had a little rodeo for the kids and I knew this was where I wanted to live. Then the next winter my dad took my brother and me to Taos to ski. I kept a little photo album and I used to caption all my Kodak Instamatic pictures. I've got a photo of a broken down adobe outside of Arroyo Seco, below the ski valley, and on it I had written 'MY FUTURE HOME.' I was enamored of the whole Western thing."

As we will see, Kim's visions of what she wants have a way of coming true. It may take a bit of time, but eventually they manifest themselves in physical form.

Being enamored of "the whole Western thing," Kim transferred from Illinois Wesleyan University to Arizona State at Tempe, where she met her first husband, an aspiring actor. When she was pregnant with their first child they debated the pros and cons of relocation. Manhattan offered theatrical opportunities, but it was a city of strangers and uncertain employment prospects. Taos, on the other hand, held both friends and job offers and it was well west of the Mississippi. The Instamatic snapshot, now a decade old, proved prophetic. They moved to Taos.

Once they were here it didn't take Kim long to get herself a horse.

"I went into the co-op in El Prado and asked a woman in the checkout line where I could find a horse to ride. As it turned out she had an insane Palomino mare named Rain. I was young and fearless and we would ride balls out on the mesa, which didn't have any houses back then. But Rain was super skittish; if a leaf blew across the road she would just lose her mind. My two boys were still little and my farrier told me the horse was a hazard to them so regretfully I sold her.

"My second horse, a blue roan, I got from Pam MacArthur. She was a very spirited competitive trail horse and also a bit headstrong. But I kept her until I was involved in a horrible automobile accident in 1998. I was so psychologically traumatized that I knew didn't have the energy to care for a horse during the winter so I gave her to a local woman who cared for her.

"A few years passed though and I started getting the horse bug again. I saw Jenny Lancaster riding in a field. She was six months pregnant and needed someone to exercise her horses so I offered to do it without pay. I rode many horses during that year to help her work out their kinks before they were sold. And then Nugget came along."

Nugget, as his name suggests, was a golden horse, a blonde sorrel. Kim, having been indelibly imprinted at age six by Roy Roger's palomino, immediately liked his looks.

"I rode Nugget for a month and he had a few little quirks. He was part Arab and hated water. Then Jenny announced she had a buyer for him in Santa Fe and I literally had this clenching in my chest. I couldn't let this horse go. But I didn't have the money to buy him."

But Kim's mother did. By then she had become a seasoned horse owner because Kim's younger sister, who also had inherited the maternal horse gene, had turned into a serious competitive rider.

"I ran home and called my mother and said, 'Do you want to buy a horse?' and she said 'Sure.' By Eastern standards horses out here are dirt-cheap and Jenny made me the deal of the century because she saw that I had totally fallen in love with this horse. So my mom bought Nugget and I'd call her after I entered him in local shows and say, 'Your horse just won a blue ribbon.'"

Nugget proved to be the horse of Kim's dreams. True, he didn't like water and he was initially quite prejudiced against trailers, but he had a dependability and business-like attitude that were exactly the qualities Kim wanted in a mount. Better yet, they communicated well with one another.

"We just had this very strong connection. I felt like we understood each other. I never had to encourage him to go or to slow down; he knew exactly when to speed up or just walk or trot. We each knew what the other was thinking. He totally took care of me. He was steady and constant and that's what I liked about him. He could be a little goofy going back to the trailer and the first year I had him, when he was only eight, we had our moments. But I knew what to expect from him and I really appreciated that."

Steadiness and predictability may have been particularly important to Kim because as a counselor and co-creator of DreamTree Project, Inc. a transitional living program for youth at risk, she encountered enough unsteadiness and unpredictability in her day job. Moreover, her night job, as a singer/songwriter responsible for a band, involved a demanding schedule of performances and intense social interaction.

"I'm always around people and I love it, but it requires a lot of personal energy. Getting on Nugget and heading out into the mountains was my therapy. A lot of the ladies I rode with liked to hang together and talk. I'd stay behind or go ahead because for me it was a time to not be social for a change."

The one topic on which Kim and Nugget did not agree at all was trailers. So Kim, true to her professional training, called in the equine equivalent of a therapist: an animal communicator.

"Even after I got Nugget, it was a big pain in the ass to get him in a trailer. I tried everything I knew and I was at my wits end. Jeff, our accountant at DreamTree, mentioned that he was an animal communicator. Well, I live in Taos. I'm open minded about things like that. So I said, 'Come talk to my horse' and Jeff explains that he works in concepts and images, not words. He comes out and asks Nugget what's up with not getting in the trailer and Nugget lets him know that he hates the sound of the trailer when he walks into it. Now I've already put in rubber mats and done everything I could to make the trailer comfortable, so I ask Jeff to explain that there is nothing more I can do, and if Nugget wants to get to the trails he loves so much he is going to have to get into this moveable box. So Jeff did just that and I swear to God, Nugget jumped in the trailer from that day on. I am not making this up!

"Then Jeff asked me if there was anything else I wanted to know about Nugget and I said just ask him what his thing is, you know, what turns him on. So Jeff did and Nugget responded that he just wants to be a horse. He doesn't want to be a show pony or police horse or anything fancy. He's just happy to be a horse and be there for me."

Unfortunately Kim was not destined to have Nugget with her for as long as she expected. When he was fifteen, he began colicking frequently. After extensive and expensive tests and treatments, the cause was discovered to be terminal liver disease.

"Even in the last few days before his death we had this connection. I sat on the ground beside him and his eyeball was to my eyeball and we very much knew and understood each other. He let me know when it was time to go. I called Bessie [Bessie Babits, Taos' equine vet] and she and the backhoe guy came out and he dug this huge grave. And I led Nugget over there….it was heartbreaking.

"We buried him in the corner of the field behind my house, and for three days my boarder horse and my donkey held vigil at the grave. They laid on it, pawed at it and rolled on it. They slept on it and they stopped eating. The boarder horse would let out this long whinny that sounded like crying. I had never seen or heard anything like that kind of mourning.

"I didn't think I would ever have a horse again. Nugget was that significant to me. But then spring came and my friends were all going riding and people were offering me their horses to ride, which I appreciated. I started to open up to the idea of getting another horse. I didn't want to actively look for one. I just told myself if a horse came along I would be open to it, but I didn't expect anything to happen very soon.

"Ironically, at this point my mother comes into it again. Shortly after Nugget died my mother happened to go to an exhibit at the Field Museum in Chicago on the origins of the horse. She walked into the gift shop and found this little blonde horse fetish with little turquoise feet and sent it to me in honor of Nugget. So I put it on my altar in the bedroom and started thinking, what if there could be another golden horse in my life? But then I think, I don't want to get locked into a color; I just want the right horse to show up.

"So it sat on my altar for a while and then I get a call from Jenny Lancaster saying, 'I'm bringing two horses in, one is a black and white paint and you are not going to believe it, but the other is a palomino.' She brings them home and turns them out in the field in fifty-mile-per-hour winds and I watch the palomino run. He's not showy and prancey like Nugget; he's a big barrel-chested steady Quarter Horse, but I'm so mesmerized by him I don't even look at the paint.

"Prior to Jenny's calling me, once I had realized I felt open to getting a horse again, I would hear myself saying, 'I just want a horse friend again, I really want a horse friend again.' Then, about ten minutes after we had unloaded these horses and were watching them run around in the field, Jenny says, 'By the way, the paint's name is Dallas and the other guy is called Amigo.' And I was just blown away because I had probably repeated to myself a dozen times the phrase "I need a horse friend again.'

"Like Nugget, Amigo's not super affectionate. He was probably a cowboy horse; he didn't know what to do with a treat. He didn't even know what a carrot was. But like Nugget, he's a businessman. He doesn't spook, he knows his job and does it. That's what I like about him. Now we're starting to form a bond. When I get home from work he hears me and his ears perk up and he nickers and comes over to the fence to greet me. I've got a horse friend again."

SUSAN NESTOR

"You don't ever want to disrespect an animal's spirit."

Susan Nestor owns five Arabian or Arabian cross horses and nearly as many houses of diverse ancestry. The original Overland Ranch homestead is a one hundred year old, thick-walled adobe set on a mesa in Arroyo Hondo just north of Taos. The multi-bedroomed estate near Albuquerque is where Susan and her husband, Neal Meisner, raised their four children. My favorite is the ultra-modern steel-framed, glass-walled cube clinging to the side of a steep, forested hill above Taos Canyon. That's where I scheduled our interview because I have always had a passion for minimalist contemporary architecture which I don't see much of in Northern New Mexico.

This tiny gem of a home is surrounded by towering ponderosa pines, but enough trees have been cleared to allow an eagle's eye view of the wooded peaks to the south and west. The sense of solitude is profound and pervasive. It's also pretty much a given because the long winding driveway to the house is more suitable for mountain goats than automobiles. The only neighbors who drop in unannounced tend to be four-legged: elk, bears, and the occasional mountain lion.

In addition to maintaining this mountain hideaway, which involves plowing that formidable driveway with an ATV in the winter, Susan oversees a hay farm near the Colorado border and several rental properties. And then there's the livestock: the afore-mentioned horses, three alpacas, and a couple of Great Pyrenees to guard everyone. Managing all this, plus keeping up with four adult children and three grandchildren and giving refresher CPR courses for local firemen, requires highly developed organizational skills and a lot of stamina. When friends describe Susan as "high energy," they're making a gross understatement.

The energy and drive were very likely present from birth, but when Susan was sixteen an encounter with a runaway horse gave her the confidence and determination to transcend the narrowly traditional expectations for women in the small southern Ohio community where she was born and raised.

"I was a pretty unhappy teenager living at home, but a church camp about 200 miles away needed a lifeguard. They had horses, which I had always loved although I had no riding lessons at all. My family was very poor and we didn't have a lot of options and I was certainly not ever going to be able to have a horse. But I did have a few wealthy friends with horses who had given me some tips.

"So the first experience I had at that camp was when the local farm boys put me on a horse and slapped her on the butt. We went flying over hill and dale and even jumped two fences. I stayed on. I wasn't going to let those boys get the best of me. Besides, if I'd fallen off I'd probably have been killed. When we finally got back they hooted and hollered and said, 'We forgot to tell you. She doesn't stop very well.'

"Right then I made it my goal to ride that horse. By the end of the summer we were very good friends and that horse stopped for me. The horses at the camp gave me confidence. I think learning to control the unstoppable horse gave me a sense that I could do whatever I wanted.

"One of the things I wanted was to get away from where I was, but not more than a dozen girls from my high school graduating class of 1970 went to college; it was very backward in southern Ohio. But I thought, 'Nobody's going to hold me back. I don't need anyone's money and I don't need anyone's support. I WILL go to college.' So when I graduated high school a year early I got a job and went off to Ohio State. I studied English, but part way through I discovered the ag school so I minored in agriculture. But I still couldn't afford a horse. It just wasn't going to happen."

Fast forward twenty or so years. Susan has gone to law school, married Neal, and the two of them have left "the dark and gloom of northern Ohio" for New Mexico. They've done well investing in real estate, Neal's commercial painting business is thriving, and they have raised four children, the youngest of whom is a horse-crazy girl. Horses are finally going to happen.

"We were living in the mountains east of Albuquerque and Lily, who was about ten, fell in love with the neighbor's horses and of course I encouraged her big time. We finally bought one of them, Buddy, for her eleventh birthday. The former owners mentioned that he was a registered Arabian, and I did some research and discovered a Cinderella story. He was from famous bloodlines out of Mallorca, Spain, and the breeders had lost track of him, but they had always wondered what happened to him because he was so beautiful even when he was young. I registered him so Lily could join the youth Arabian club and get some help. We were both novices, learning together. I didn't want Lily to be riding around by herself so I got a twenty-five-year-old half-Arab and we did a lot of riding together, which gave me some confidence to get back into horses after not riding since being run around the hills of southern Ohio by a horse that wouldn't stop."

Buddy, the neighbor's backyard horse, surprised Susan with his illustrious origins. But that wasn't the only remarkable thing about him. As Susan tells it, "At some point I kind of knew that Buddy was an angel. It was his smell. It was definitely different from the other horses. There's something about it; it's sweet. And he always has eagles around him. At the Hondo ranch an eagle lived in the pasture with him and even when we rode several miles away we would look up and the eagle would be there. Once when we were at Cebolla Mesa, five eagles played with us the whole ride, soaring up and down the Gorge, teasing us in a friendly way. Then this year, when I brought Buddy up to our place in Taos Canyon, two eagles appeared as we turned him loose in the pasture. They played and danced like spirits sent from God. Those eagles stayed until I took him down to Albuquerque during the hard snows and I haven't seen them since. I know that I need to bring Buddy back to Taos Canyon soon or he will get depressed because he needs his eagle spirits.

"I also know Buddy understands when you talk to him and he takes care of people. Once Lily ran across a rattlesnake and he just stood there, then backed up of his own accord because she wasn't doing anything about it. He didn't panic at all. Another time when I was riding him we also came across a rattlesnake. It was about ten feet away and he backed me up into a tree and pretty much forced me to get off. Then he spun around, killed the rattler and stood stock-still, waiting for me to get back on him.

"I believe angels are sent from God, or whatever you want to call it, to help someone or to change a course of action. Buddy changed the whole course of Lily's life and probably mine too. Lily got involved in the Arab association and started showing Buddy in trail events. A couple of people told her he wasn't good enough to show and that pissed her off. So she did a lot of fitness work and training with him and eventually won the Arabian Junior Nationals. And now she's at Colorado State in vet school."

When Susan tells me she believes that horses can embody angelic presences, I'm momentarily taken aback. I've always thought of her as the ultimate pragmatist, an impressively competent manger of all things material, mechanical, and financial. But as the interview continues, she reveals a part of herself that surprises me, a part that is probably the source of her ability to handle horses and just about everything else in her busy life. The revelation unfolds as we are talking about Parade Girl, an Arabian/Hackney pony cross that Susan bought for her daughter.

"We bought PG for Lily to show. She was green and the owners were afraid of her and when we got her home she just blew up coming out of the trailer. She dumped Neal, she dumped Lily, she was skittish about everything. Then she got pigeon fever and developed a big gaping wound in her belly that drained fluid. It had to be irrigated with a garden hose every day. Being with her so much, I saw a different look in her eyes. It may have been that the illness slowed her down, or that look may have been there all along, hidden behind her craziness. So we started to talk and we made friends. She had to trust me or she was going to die.

"She lost two hundred pounds. You could see her ribs and she looked a fright. I hand fed her morning and night and she started to follow me around the yard. As she got stronger I took her on walks outside our ranch in Arroyo Hondo. There are a lot of stimuli there, crazy dogs barking at you, cows charging the fence, cars roaring by. She really gave her all to be out there with me and it made her stronger. By the time she was strong enough for me to get on her she was quite desensitized. I rode her in the same areas that we had walked and she really, really tried to be good for me."

Like Kim Treiber-Thompson, Susan Nestor uses the term "friends" to describe her horses. This isn't a term that is frequently encountered in the horse world, in which the notion of establishing dominance over one's horse, gently or by brute force, is paramount. Friendship is a far more egalitarian state. It implies the conscious recognition of the horse as a sentient being of equal worth to oneself, with thoughts and feelings that need to be taken into account. That doesn't mean abdicating control when control is needed, but it does mean acknowledging that the horse as well as the human has something to say about whatever is going on and it is worth listening to. One may not agree, but one must listen.

Susan came to this way of relating to horses when the conventional natural horsemanship technique of training through pressure and release failed miserably with PG.

"I decided I wanted to talk to PG's spirit. When I was first having trouble with her my father was visiting and he told me how he spoke to the spirit of a plow horse his family had on their farm in West Virginia. This horse, Bessie, was just impossible. She'd run off with the plow, which is a terrible problem when your survival depends on tilling the soil. But my father spoke to Bessie's spirit and got her to work for him, although she wouldn't work for anyone else. He told me to find what gave PG inner peace because then she would do anything for me

"I did this by looking into her eyes and talking to her as if I were praying, as if I were speaking directly to God. Of course I wasn't, but it was with the same kind of intense need to find a way to channel communication. I couldn't always find that channel, but when I did she had a calmness that came back to me the same way a calmness comes to you after a prayer. At those times I could do some training, like solving her issues about the trailer.

"Sometimes it took a while to establish a connection, but I would tell myself, 'We're having a difficult moment, but it isn't going to stay a difficult moment. I am going to be patient and I am going to talk to this horse's spirit.' And I believed that it would work. I believed that I would see an opening in her eye that would allow me in. That's all I did. I just sort of said a prayer, like when I saw a mountain lion under our front porch up here and I looked in her eyes and I knew she wasn't going to attack me."

This kind of communion with horses took Susan back to what she describes as "that spot from my childhood where there was the simplicity of nature and the simplicity of absolute faith." She explains that spot as follows:

"I grew up with the same kind of mystery about communicating with animals that Native Americans have, but in my case it was the old Appalachian way, the very, very old Biblical Christian teachings about living at one with the land. My grandmothers and aunts and uncles could channel to heal or to tame an animal and they could do that pretty readily. If someone was bleeding they would call my grandmother and she would lay her hands on the person and do a meditative chant and the bleeding would stop. Faith healing was commonplace and it translated into dealings with the animal kingdom. You never kill something you don't eat; you don't challenge an animal. You look at their eyes and they look at your eyes. The eyes are the windows to the soul and you don't want the soul to be diseased.

"I feel like any kind of regime or dogma when it comes to animals or people just doesn't work very well. Believing in just one way of doing things doesn't make sense. I've raised four children and some I had to be sterner with than others. Just like with some horses you might have to be a little dominant to get their attention if they're not listening to you. With others, being dominant would kill their spirit. You don't ever want to disrespect an animal's spirit. Animals are sent to us for a reason and we need to acknowledge and respect that."

That sounds to me like a great concluding sentence for my interview and I turn the recorder off and reluctantly prepare to leave the peaceful solitude of the mountains and return to town. Susan tells me to wait; she wants to tell me something more, something about the kind of thing that can happen when, as she puts it, "you seek communion with the higher order of things."

"I was riding PG in the forest above Red River shortly after my dad died and I was desperately missing him. He loved elk and I thought, 'I really need to see an elk; it would be like seeing my dad's face.' I started petting PG and I told her, 'PG, if we're going to see any elk today we need to do something. Let's talk to God a little bit; even the wind and the waves obey Him.' I swear it had been dead calm our entire ride, but just then the wind picked up and started blowing wildly and an entire herd of elk walked across a meadow in front of us. And I thought, 'Yes, that's why I'm here.'"

CHRISTINE MOREHART

"I think horses live in our world and in another dimension too."

Shortly after I'd moved my newly-purchased three-year-old gelding, Chance, into the little horse facility I'd built on my two acres, I heard that a woman from Aspen had moved into the historic John Young Hunter estate down the road from my place. I was intrigued because my then-husband and I had once considered purchasing this property. I had been enthralled by the idea of living in a house owned by one of the famous painters from Taos' glory days. However, we didn't make an offer because, like many old adobes, the house needed extensive work. I was impressed that a single woman would take on this glamorous but high-maintenance piece of real estate.

But what was even more interesting was the fact that this mysterious stranger had brought two horses with her and erected a seventy-foot round pen in John Young Hunter's former front yard. This was clearly someone I needed to know because I had been advised that round-penning was the only way to rid my new gelding of his rebellious streak. (Bad advice, as it turned out, but it took me a while to discover that.)

So when I encountered a statuesque woman with an abundant fall of remarkably mane-like dark blonde hair trotting down Piedmont Road on a fine-looking buckskin mare, I made sure to introduce myself, my horse, and my need for a round pen. And that's how I met Christine Morehart, who was to become a good friend as well as the owner of a conveniently located training venue.

Taos turned out to be a way station for Christine; the siren call of the great mother mountain was a false alarm for her. Our little town was just a bit too dusty, funky and primitive for this former Coloradan, and after a year in Mr. Hunter's house she moved to Galisteo, just outside Santa Fe. However, Taos was an important way station, a place where, like many other wounded souls who are drawn here, she recovered from a trauma, in this case a painful divorce, and pulled her life together. Most notably, she applied herself to developing a personal growth program for women that uses the horse's remarkable ability to serve as a mirror of a person's inner states.

This program, HorseContinuum, is the end product of Christine's long but peripheral involvement with horses, an involvement that became serious only when her daughter Moorea developed an interest in hunter-jumpers and dressage. It was then that Christine was inspired to learn more about equine and human psychology and eventually to venture off the trails and into the show ring. The story begins long ago and far away.

"My husband and I had a farm in New Zealand where we'd go in the northern hemisphere winter and a ranch in East Glacier, Montana for the summer. There's nothing there but wilderness. We'd go out on the trail and there would be grizzly poop, black bear poop and moose poop everywhere. We'd take our son, who wasn't even a year old, in the backpack and we'd stop for lunch and eat huckleberries off the bushes. It was a wild life! Later we bought a farm outside Aspen; it was essentially a one-room cabin. That's where I raised my two kids for fourteen years. We had a hundred acres of hay fields and about twenty semi-trained Quarter Horses. But all we did was trail ride until my daughter got into showing. Then I learned to trailer and we travelled all over three states to shows. For almost five years I watched her train and compete. I was the typical mother having a nervous breakdown on the sidelines during the shows."

Christine had no interest in participating in showing at that point. She considered herself too "right brained and introverted" to withstand the pressures of competition. Rather, she was drawn to the emerging field of equine-assisted therapy. So after her tempestuous twenty-year marriage to a man she describes as "very attractive and very high-powered" came to an end, she created HorseContinuum to help women explore and transcend personal issues through their relationships with horses. She bought a four-year-old Parelli-trained Quarter Horse mare to use in the program, and also requisitioned the services of her daughter's former mount, an older thoroughbred gelding.

The mare, Contessa, had been schooled within an inch of her life, but nevertheless she presented Christine with an unexpected challenge that forced her to reevaluate the way she dealt with horses.

"I think Contessa was over trained. I think she felt overly pressured. I noticed from the beginning that her canter was incorrect and uncomfortable. She could trot perfectly collected, but when we cantered she just freaked out and bucked unless we were on the straightaway going uphill. But now our relationship has become so profoundly deep that I don't focus on cantering or training any more. That's not her thing. She's a relationship horse. When we moved to the house in Galisteo we just rode out. Just the two of us; she didn't need any other horses along. We did this thing I call 'Precipice Valley Viewing.' I would give her full rein and just go with her and she'd take me to the highest point around and then just stand there and look over this entire panoramic valley for forty-five minutes or so. And I'd be hugging her neck or just sitting there meditating. I was still going through stuff about my divorce and I'd talk to her and we had this extraordinary communication with measurable positive effects. She became very happy and very trustworthy. I lost my relationship with my husband, but I developed a real relationship with my horse.

"I went to a pet psychic who told me that Contessa wanted to do tricks, she didn't want to canter and gallop and all that other stuff. So I got a book on teaching tricks and a pedestal and ball and taught her all the tricks I could. Now people come to the arena when I'm not around and tell me she runs to the pedestal and does tricks on her own. I stopped trying to make her do what I wanted and went along with what she enjoyed."

When Christine dropped her agenda and started listening to her horse, Contessa was happier and their somewhat rocky relationship became easy and joyful. Something else happened too. The prospect of entering a show ring and being judged became less daunting. Christine discovered her inner competitor.

"After four years here I got tired of just riding out. I found I had a drive to do more of a performance thing. For my birthday my daughter gave me a dressage lesson with a German trainer who had been helping me with Contessa before we stopped training her. And one day over at the dressage barn in El Dorado I saw a woman with a big Hanoverian gelding and it was like being at those horse shows with my daughter all those years ago when I was so amazed at these fearless women on their big horses. And I thought, 'Oh my God, what would it be like to have a horse like that?'"

Christine and the trainer ended up buying a three-year-old mare, Madizen, whom Christine describes as "a big black enormous horse who didn't know anything."

"Madizen was completely green, but had a sweet and very mellow spirit. She felt completely safe. I realized that she was not like Contessa. Madizen is a left-brained horse that you have to motivate and be very provocative with, unlike a right-brained horse that requires you to stay calm. And after I got Madizen I discovered that there's a left-brained extrovert in me too. We're just like our horses."

Christine put Madizen and herself into training at the dressage barn and found, for herself at least, that the challenge of learning a more precise and disciplined way of riding was actually fun as well as "just horrible, so hard." Enough people commented on Madizen's innate talent for dressage that Christine entered her in some schooling shows—but with the trainer rather than herself aboard.

Then, at the end of 2010, Christine mounted her big horse and entered the show ring for the first time.

"It was so scary. You come into the arena and this classically trained British guy is talking about your horse and its height and everything. I wasn't that experienced, but Madizen was so kind and had so much heart that she took care of me even though the trainer had thought I shouldn't ride her because she had been acting up that morning. But my daughter had come all the way from California to braid her mane so I was determined to ride. Then after I did the introductory level and had the time of my life I realized that it was really fun to compete. I had never done anything like that before and I wasn't even as nervous as I thought I would be even though I used to just die when I watched my daughter in the show ring."

But nothing ever stays the same. While Christine got over her performance anxiety, Madizen completely lost her cool.

"After a year and four months living at the dressage barn everything shifted for her. She became right-brained, flighty, spooky, not even wanting to be touched. I couldn't ride her, only the trainer could and even then there was a lot of fighting. We brought in internationally acclaimed vets, we tried everything. People said it was a hormonal thing, a Hanoverian thing, but I felt so helpless because I couldn't fix her. An alternative vet I consulted asked me if she'd had any shots right before her personality changed and I remembered that she had gotten a flu/rhino vaccination, which might just be a coincidence. Or maybe not.

"At any rate, I decided to give her the winter off. I brought her home to my big corral with a shelter she could go in and out of as she pleased. After three days here she started to become her old self. I gave her a lot of natural supplements and a lot of nurturance and I was able to ride her in only a few weeks. Now she's happy and she loves Contessa. I'm not taking her back into the dressage world until she's more balanced in herself and able to handle it. She needs emotional support and physical contact and space. She didn't get that in the dressage barn. She had been taken away from her family in a large corral and put in a stall with a tiny run. She couldn't even touch another horse. She became so imbalanced there that she kicked a hole in the wall and tried to kick the vet. Everyone called her the drama queen. And this was a horse that had formerly been calm and confident."

Fortunately Christine was herself sufficiently calm and confident to follow her instincts. She saw that Madizen's problems were largely due to a restrictive and unnatural environment and she moved her into a healthier situation.

"Now having Madizen home I'm doing what I love, building rapport, respect, and a connection of a kind you would never expect you could have with a different species. It gives you so much insight into yourself and your own ability to live in joy. People don't understand how much they are missing by not understanding the creatures we live with and how we are connected to them and to everything else. And how much love is there when you open to these creatures. It doesn't matter whether it's a horse or an elephant or a dolphin, but horses are truly amazing. Their prey animal survival instinct creates the ability to understand our inner states and reveal them to us. They really can read our energetics.

"Actually, I think horses live in our world and in another dimension too, and they do this by simply living in the moment. I am so blessed, so fortunate, to have created something in my life that gives me more than I ever dreamt of. I am just so grateful for my life with horses."

JENNIFER SIEGEL

"Horses are like the juice of life. Without them my spirit would dry up."

I was mucking out Chance's paddock one summer day when a gray Toyota Tundra pulled off Piedmont Road into the semicircular drive that serves my little horse facility A very thin, youngish woman wearing running clothes and a baseball hat hopped out. "Hi," she said. "My name's Jennifer. I'm new in the neighborhood and I've got a horse. Where do you ride around here?"

That was my introduction to Dr. Jennifer Siegel, an emergency room doctor and refugee from the congestion, confusion, and combustion fumes of Los Angeles. A few weeks later I met her Polish Arabian gelding Hoolie, who got on well with Chance, and we had a companionable ride on the trails adjacent to my property.

Jennifer told me that she'd done a lot of "ride and tie," a rough and tumble cross country sport involving teams of one horse and two people who alternate riding and running a predetermined course. It's sufficiently challenging to man and beast alike that merely completing the course is considered a win. However, I knew little else about her equine activities until we sat down in my living room and I turned on my recorder and documented an amazing life story: a tale of two mothers, a wild child, and the passion for horses that bound them all together.

"I grew up in the hills of Los Angeles, in Mandeville Canyon, and I always loved animals and plants. When I was in grade school my mom bought me *Misty of Chincoteague* and the Black Stallion books and t-shirts with horses on them. She loved horses. I have photos of her riding with her friends in the Bay Area, where she grew up. She was about six feet tall, a lovely, beautiful lady and her nickname was 'Tex.'

"When I was in grade school my parents divorced. Our life was chaotic and I was miserable. I ran away from home several times to escape the tension. One of my friends had wealthy parents with a horse ranch in Topanga Canyon and that became a refuge for me. I felt at home sitting in the hay, smelling the horses. My dad would take me up there to ride. But eventually there were problems with the managers of the ranch and the kids who rode there took over, or at least we thought we did. We rode all the ranch horses whenever we wanted. I didn't really know anything, but I'd go into the corrals and look the horses in the eyes and just get on them and ride. I was about ten years old then and it all felt completely natural and easy.

"Then Diane, the woman who was to become my foster mom, showed up as the new manager of the ranch. She had a lot of horse experience, breaking colts, training and showing and jumping and trail riding. She was about twenty-five when I met her, but she seemed really old to me at the time. When she came on the scene I thought, who the hell are you, trying to tell me what to do, and I had a fistfight with her. She pinned me down and laughed while I was struggling and wishing I were stronger so I could throw her off me. So she showed me who was boss, and then she said, 'I'll tell you what. I'll teach you to ride under one condition. You have to go to school.' Because I'd been ditching school. And I said, 'Deal!' because all I wanted was to be around horses. It was my only pleasure in life. I found safety in the beingness of horses. They were these big warm beasts who were always accepting and if you just want to hang out with them, that's what they liked. If you didn't have an agenda, it was fine. They smell wonderful, they're funny and interesting and I could just watch them for hours, looking at their eyelashes, the hair in their ears, the swirls on their noses. I felt if I could go to sleep on the back of a horse, or in the stall with one, I could truly rest.

"At first Diane would help me travel back and forth from my house to the ranch, but I wanted to be at the ranch all the time. I was really unhappy at home. So I kept running away to get there and having huge fights with my real mom. Finally, Diane asked her to let me live with her at the ranch. My mom was upset, but she knew she couldn't handle me so she reluctantly said okay. I lived at the ranch from then on.

"Later my mom was really happy about it because it turned out to be so good for me. In my mind, my family had fallen apart. My older sister was already in trouble. She was gone most of the time and had no interest in me and I felt so alone without her. I remember thinking I don't want to get in trouble too. But I also remember being at a party drunk and stoned and the cops coming in a helicopter to break it up. I remember how they shined a bright light in my face and asked where my parents were and how I broke away from them and ran all the way home. Fortunately, Diane took me on and she was powerful and loving at the same time. I think she could tell that I had some potential, but I was going down a bad road the way I was. But I don't blame my mother for that. She had four kids, a new boyfriend with three kids, and had to go to court repeatedly to get child support from my father.

"So I went from being a wild, crazy, ballsy kid to being responsible for sixty horses. I fed them twice a day, cleaned their stalls, and exercised some of them. There was a riding club that used the ranch's horses and my best friend Kiki and I got the horses ready for the club rides. We would take them out of the pen riding bareback and having six horses on either side of us. It was really wild, but great fun. Of course Diane would always yell at us and tell us to take them one at a time and we would ignore her. We'd saddle them for the club members and then take the tack off and clean the horses after they were finished. It was a big responsibility and I loved it. I wanted someone to give me boundaries. I loved my mom, who was a free spirit, but I knew I needed structure.

"Diane was really good about providing it. Horses are dangerous. You can't do just anything with a horse, but I thought I could. Diane taught me about all the "wrecks," as she called them, that could happen if you weren't careful. I was a perceptive and sensitive kid and I learned fast to be super aware all the time of myself and what was going on with the horse. Now it's automatic with me. I watch their ears, listen to their breathing, and stay in touch with every movement."

Unfortunately the Topanga Canyon ranch interlude ended after two years, when Diane, her husband Ken, their baby daughter, and Jennifer moved to a small town near San Luis Obispo. The family dynamic underwent a radical change, and not for the better.

"We lived in a little house on five acres with the horses we brought from Topanga. One of them was mine, a sorrel Quarter Horse named Skipper. He had come from the racetrack and was insane because of his experiences there, full of pizazz and really spooky. Any time he was around any excitement he would freak out. I entered him in a halter class at a fair and he broke out in a sweat and spun and stomped. I have a picture of myself in my Future Farmers of America jacket and white pants and boots with a horrible frown on my face leading him out of the show ring. I was pissed off that I had such a crazy horse when everyone else had expensive, well-trained show horses.

"After we moved, things didn't go so well. Ken had stayed in Los Angeles to work and only came home on weekends and this was hard on Diane. I had been the main barn girl in Topanga, but now she wouldn't let me have anything to do with any of the horses except my own. Eventually Child Protective Services removed me from the house. The day I left I was given my clothes in a bag and the show halter I'd gotten for my birthday, but not the new show saddle that I had worked all summer to buy. Ken said, 'You ride like a sack of potatoes. We're not giving it to you. It's ours.'

"So I left with my horse. I was about fifteen at the time. The principal of my high school had volunteered to take me in and Child Protective Services had okayed that. But within two weeks his wife and daughter wanted me out and there was an ugly scene with them yelling at me while I was working with my horse and then the wife yelling at her husband and demanding a divorce. So I say, 'I've had it with you guys,' and get on my horse—because my horse is always my solution—and ride down the road to the house of one of my teachers and ask him what to do. He tells me to go over to the Stuart's house. Mr. Stuart was my math teacher and I had a good relationship with him because I was a math whiz and I babysat for his family. His wife and kids were great too.

"So I ride a couple of miles over there which I can because we're in a rural farm area, and say, 'Russ, I can't live with those people. They're nuts. Can I stay here?' And he says, 'Sure. You can put your horse in with our pony, but you have to follow some rules. You go to school, you take good care of your animals, and you go to church on Sundays.' Now I'm Jewish, but I say okay to church on Sundays. So I stayed there until I graduated from high school. They were really sweet people."

Although Jennifer's relationship with her foster mother had been disrupted (it was subsequently repaired and they are close friends today) the loving discipline Diane, had imposed on her rebellious young charge had a positive and permanent effect which lasts to this day.

"Diane taught me to never quit. She wouldn't let me say 'I can't.' She instilled in me a work ethic I benefit from to this day. In Future Farmers of America there's something called 'project competition.' All the rich kids used to win because they would show their million dollar sheep or cows that their parents had bought them. I told my teachers that I wanted to enter it and they sort of snickered, like, 'what do *you* have to show?' And I said, 'I have a lot. I have a rabbit project'—I sold rabbits and rabbit meat to make money—'a replacement heifer, a horse, laying hens, a sow with piglets, and a job.' By this time I had a little teeny Toyota truck my real mom, Carol Larney, had bought me and a job working at a huge horse ranch about five miles away. I did everything, drove the tractor, bucked the hay, moved horses, cleaned stalls. I was Little Miss Barn Hand and I was in heaven.

"So I told my teachers I didn't care what they thought, I was entering the competition. And my project was perfect. My barn was spotless and my records were impeccable. The day comes that we go to see the results of the competition and there were all these rich kids there expecting to win and I'm going, 'Yeah, whatever, I don't even know why I'm here," and then they announced the winner and said my name and I was shocked. I was the poor kid with nothing and they picked me. I think what the judges really admired was the fact that I'd done the project all by myself with no help from my parents or anybody else.

"After high school I went on to Cal Poly to study animal science. I wanted to be a horse vet. But I did my first year of animal science and it wasn't sufficiently challenging. I'm learning about milking cows and shearing sheep and I want to do math and science and chemistry. I've always been a scientist, ever since I was a kid. My dad was a geneticist at UCLA and he had me separating drosophila [fruit flies used in genetic experiments] under the microscope when I was in third grade.

"So I changed my major to biochemistry while I worked with small animal and horse vets in my spare time. But I found lameness exams and cattle vaccinations and pregnancy tests and artificial insemination boring. And a lot of people told me I was too small to be a vet and I believed them. But the real problem was that I found veterinary medicine somewhat limiting; I wanted to do more science.

"Then someone told me that I didn't have to be a vet to be around animals. If I went into human medicine I could afford to own as many animals as I wanted. So I said 'Okay, that sounds good,' and I went to medical school. Decisions come easily when you're young."

Not only when you're young, but also when serendipitous events make it clear that the Great Mother Mountain wants you in Taos. After medical school and residency, Jennifer moved back to Los Angeles to pursue her career. Once again she found herself living in Topanga Canyon, scene of her youthful escapades, but this time with her own horse, a finely bred Polish Arabian. However Topanga's proximity to the Los Angeles megalopolis was a major drawback.

"I had been looking to move out of LA for two years. I wanted to be somewhere I could have some acreage and ride in the hills and be in nature. My boyfriend and I had been looking in Colorado, Wyoming, and Idaho and then one day he says to me,' Look at this ad for Taos. It's a magical place.' I had never been to Taos, but all of a sudden I'm sitting in my car talking on the phone to the director of the emergency department at Holy Cross. I didn't think anything was going to come of it. Then I really listened to what he had to say and it sounded so perfect. So we drove out and interviewed and I liked everybody I met and they hired both of us just like that."

Hoolie, the Polish Arabian, came to Taos with Jennifer and the move signaled a shift in their relationship. Together they had done well enough in the ride and tie events that Jennifer's competitive nature was satisfied. But Hoolie had suffered a bout of laminitis that left him prone to lameness. It was time for something new, and for a second horse who would be consistently rideable. Jennifer purchased an Egyptian Arabian, a more dominant, confident horse than Hoolie, whom she describes as the kind of horse who says, "Let me climb in your lap and nuzzle you because I'm insecure." More importantly, at Diane's suggestion, Jennifer discovered the work of Klaus Ferdinand Hempfling, a proponent of working with horses from a place of Zen-like inner stillness, a place where respecting the horse's point of view comes naturally.

"I used to be a person with an agenda. Now I've learned to drop the agenda and play with my horses. When I do that our relationship is infinitely better. I'll go out on a windy day to ride and maybe the horse is frisky. He wants to run free and fast. So I'll dismount, take the tack off, and tell him to go. Then I get the other horse out and let him run too. Sometimes I run with them, sometimes I chase them, sometimes they chase me."

"I can't imagine a life without horses. Taking care of and being with my horses is right up there with eating on my list of things to do everyday. They are the juice of life. Without them my spirit would dry up."

Our formal interview comes to an abrupt end because Jennifer is needed at the hospital, but she calls me later to add a final observation that she feels is important.

"We all seek a relationship with our horses. We're all seekers, trying to learn more.

But we learn a little and then we're experts and criticize everyone who doesn't do things our way. A know-it-all attitude stops people from growing and it does harm to people and horses alike. I wish horse people were more humble. I think our horses would like that too."

Saved by Horses

Jenny Lancaster

Tamee Zimmerman

Karen Soomekh

Sandra Miller

SAVED BY HORSES

"Horses change lives. They give young people confidence and self-esteem. They produce peace and tranquility for troubled souls—they give us hope."
—Toni Robinson

JENNY LANCASTER

"Training wild horses and raising a family are what I've chosen to do. I have an obligation to give them both the best life possible and not to ruin them or force them into something to make me look good."

Jenny Lancaster waves her hand at a bookcase built into the wall of her family room. "That's the self-help section." Sure enough, it's filled with books on personal growth and spiritual evolution. She turns to another wall. "Over there's a photo of my grandmother on a pony when she was a little girl. My mother and father both rode too. And those are some trophies Teva, my nine-year-old, won a couple of years ago. And here's a picture of me and my husband, Humie, getting married on horseback down by the Rio Grande Gorge."

Continuing the home tour, Jenny steers me toward the children's wing after pointing out a display of carefully framed paintings documenting six-year-old Oz's evolution as a fledgling artist. Both Teva and Oz have spacious bedrooms chock full of books, models, maps, chess sets, and sports trophies, all neatly stored on shelves and tables. The array of creative and educational toys is so enticing that I have an unaccountable urge to sit down on the floor and build something out of Legos.

I've already had the outside tour, a leisurely ramble around the ten acres that make up Jenny's Diamond Horseshoe Ranch. I've seen the corrals and shelters for the horses she boards, the big round pen and the bigger arena where she works the horses she trains and sells, the pastures for turnout, and the tack shed with an array of ribbons that bear testimony to forays into every kind of equine competition imaginable: jumping, dressage, reining, and polo. Everything is in immaculate condition, from the dry footing in the arena to the poop-free corrals. I notice that despite the currently high price of hay, the feeders contain abundant quantities of high quality grass hay imported from Colorado. All in all, it's an impressive spread.

I'm even more impressed when we sit down in the living room and Jenny tells me the story of how she transformed herself from a little hippie kid into an entrepreneurial horsewoman. Those self-help books have not gone unread. I'm talking to a woman who is serious about bettering herself and creating the stable family life that she herself lacked as the child of idealistic parents who embraced the ethos—and chaos—of the sixties.

"As a kid, it seemed to me we lived like gypsies, once in a school bus, another time in a tipi, sometimes in communes with other families. We often lived without electricity or a phone, but we had gardens and organic food and a healthy life style. We never stayed anywhere very long. But everywhere we lived, whether it was Canada or upstate New York or Florida or the Caribbean, I found horses. I would do anything to ride; I would clean stalls, or work on farms. It didn't matter what kind of horse, a draft horse or a donkey, if it had four legs and ears and a trot and resembled a horse, I'd ride it. Horses were the continuity in my life and also the basis of everything I've ever done. I always felt connected to them and comfortable with them.

"My first horse was a Newfoundland pony named Shawna that I got when I was nine. My parents had divorced and my mother sent me to live with my father in Canada and he felt so guilty about the divorce that he bought me this pony. She took me so far in just two years. I lived in a wonderland of little girls and horses. Our families may not have had much money or even owned horse trailers, but we had endless fun; we would gallop bareback on our horses and fall off into the snow. And Shawna and I won every competition we entered.

"Then when I was about fourteen I went back to live with my mother who had decided she wanted to live in Puerto Rico on the beach to get away from the cold of upstate New York. I went with her and my three little siblings and we started our life all over again. I needed to earn some money so I, a little blonde girl with no Spanish, hitchhiked to the El Nuevo Comandante Racetrack in San Juan and asked for a job riding horses. I started as a walker and worked up to being an exercise girl.

"Then I met a hunter-jumper trainer from Massachusetts who rehabbed sore race horses and I went to work for him. He introduced me to a man who was starting an equestrian center on St. Martin and wanted to fly eight thoroughbreds over from Puerto Rico. So they teach me how to train the horses to get into wooden crates and board the plane and I fly over with them and help unload them and transport them to the French-speaking side of St Martin. I must have been no more than sixteen or seventeen at the time. While I was on St Martin I met a young Frenchman who worked for the owner of one of the thoroughbreds."

Jenny's voice trails off and she smiles. I can guess what's coming next. Yes, she fell in love with the young Frenchman and married him at the tender age of nineteen. This union led to eight years residence in France, during which she enrolled in the University of Lyon and became fluent in French. At the suggestion of her French mother-in-law she also went to modeling school and enjoyed a temporary career as a runway and photographic model, of which she remarks wryly, "Designers and photographers liked me because I was tall and had broad shoulders and looked good in haute couture fur coats." However, her primary focus continued to be horses. She worked at a thoroughbred breeding farm and a hunter-jumper barn, and schooled horses for the captain of France's national equestrian team. Moreover, she was a member of the first nationally competitive women's polo team in France, a fact that explains the archaic polo gear hanging beside the door of her tack room.

This glamorous ex-pat life wasn't to last, however; shortly after the amicable termination of her marriage Jenny returned to the States.

"I had been living in France with a wealthy, famous polo player boyfriend and I really wasn't comfortable in that lifestyle. I wanted my own me, my own position in life, whether it involved money or not. So I left France and went to Woodstock to live with and work for my aunt, who was a jewelry designer. I immediately got into the horse thing there and started playing polo. I also met my second husband, a jeweler and musician and we had a wonderful run of living together for a few years and getting married and having it annulled after ten months. More importantly, during that time I went to work for a steeplechase trainer from Ireland. He was hardcore, difficult to get along with, and he worked me to the bone. He'd scream at me and make me look bad so that the horses he was showing to clients would look as if anything they did wrong was my fault as a rider.

"I swore to myself if I ever taught riding that I would never ever humiliate anyone. That holds true for horse training too. You cannot make a horse angry or upset and expect to get a good result. They may do what you want, but it won't be pretty or pleasant for anyone."

Remember the self-help books? Jenny's desire to be "my own me" was never far from the surface. After her second divorce she decided that another change of locale might be the key to finding the person she was meant to be.

"I was about twenty-eight at the time and that's when I realize my life is going way too fast and I still haven't established my own identity or secured my own place. I still need to find out who Jenny is. So I remember that when I was a little hippie kid my mother and stepfather and I and my brother and sister lived for six months down by the rope bridge south of Taos in Pilar. I'm thinking I need to head back to New Mexico and see what that's all about.

"I load up my Saab convertible with my stuff and my hundred-and-forty-pound Rottweiler-Bernese Mountain Dog mix, who takes up the whole back seat, and with about fifteen dollars in my pocket I head for Santa Fe. I get there and go to the Coyote Café and I'm surrounded by Californians and New Yorkers and I want to get the hell out of there because I don't need that scene anymore. So I trek up to Taos to see the place I used to live and to stay with my girlfriend Val, who's a massage therapist. Once I'm there I see the Chet Mitchell Corral across from Cid's Market and I walk in and say, 'Hello, I'm Jenny and I really can ride. Do you have any work for me?' But I have on these lizard skin cowboy boots and I look like a real city slicker and Chet has no clue about what I can do. So I offer to work a horse for free to show him and he tells me to meet him Sunday morning and we'll go to the mountains and move some cattle. Now I don't know anything about cattle, but I go with him and do what I can on my borrowed horse and he says, 'Well, you've got a pretty good seat there. Come on over tomorrow and I've got this little Doc Bar gelding that's kinda ornery and if you can train him so I can sell him, you've got a job.' So I train the horse and three weeks later he's sold. I start working for Chet and he talks me up around town and I start getting work from other people. And in the meantime I'm using what I learned from my aunt the jeweler back in Woodstock by making concho belts and other stuff to bring in extra money."

As before, her work with horses gave Jenny's life structure and provided income. But there was still some inner work to be done.

"When I arrived in Taos, I was a lost woman trying to find herself. My girlfriend Val said, 'You know, AA is really cool. It's like free therapy.' So I go to AA and there are all these fabulous, beautiful, amazing, strong women, but I'm thinking, 'Oh my God, this is a cult. There's all this God talk and this twelve-step stuff. What have I gotten myself into?' But it started to feel good and I was making some nice friends so I went with it for a while. Now I think everybody should do the AA twelve steps. I think they should have it in schools. It was a huge gift in my life, to learn to live clean, sober, and honestly, to backtrack through my past and fix my relationships, to forgive everyone who wasn't just like I wanted them to be and to forgive myself for whatever I felt I had done wrong."

The twelve-step therapy wasn't Jenny's only self-improvement project during her early years in Taos. She saw that jumping, polo and fox hunting were hardly the disciplines of choice in northern New Mexico and she set out to learn about reining and working cows. And then a pivotal event occurred: she rode a cutting horse.

"A light bulb went off. This is the ultimate riding with your body, just laying the reins on the neck and letting the horse do its job. So I started looking into cutting and reining with the intention of finding out what I needed to learn in order to make money training horses in Taos. Also, I discovered the horse whispering techniques and I started getting into that, but only in a half-assed kind of way, reading books, working with Buck Brannaman and going to Pat Parelli. I got the message and it was a good one, to work the horse from the hoof up.

"But I still wasn't succeeding. I was helping people buy horses, but the coupling between the person and the horse wasn't working. I failed in many ways at first. I managed to buy a two-and-a-half acre piece of land and put a mobile home on it and fences and a round pen. But I reached the limit of what I knew and I needed to learn more. So I rented my house out and took out a loan and paid the best clinicians I knew—like Barbra Schulte, Craig Cameron and Al Dunning—to teach me their stuff. I took a year and a half to work with these three trainers and I came home with an entire new education. I had a whole new approach, a whole new energy about me. I knew what would work and what wouldn't and I've been building on that ever since and I'll never forget what Barbra Schulte told me. She advised me that I ever gave a clinic I should remember not to think it's about me because it's not. It's about the information I'm trying to pass on.

"Horses are a reflection of what you are and if you call yourself a trainer you have to back that up. You can't produce a horse that will do what the rider needs it to do if you don't have experience. When I was young I was very strong, confident and bossy with big energy and I could usually conquer any situation with a horse. But that wasn't the point. I was bullying my horses and making them brace against me. Horses are individuals just like us and you have to know where they are coming from.

"Now after all this extensive experience of learning different types of riding and different disciplines I can tell when a certain person needs a certain type of horse and I know how to teach that person to deal with that horse. That's my goal, to really make those partnerships work. And also to help the horse cope with the human. Finding horses for people and helping people with their horses means that you end up working on the person. Horses are easy to deal with once you know what they're going through because they're consistent. The horse isn't lying; he's just telling you where he's at, like, 'I want to bite you right now because I don't trust you.' Period. Over and out.

"But human beings are much more complex because they can be lying. Unfortunately you can't walk up to a person and say, 'This is a time to for you to be honest about what you feel' and have them actually do it. They have to figure it out for themselves. It's really hard to get a person to understand that when she gasps and jumps back because she's afraid, the horse gets scared because it's terrified of her fear. All I can do is provide the environment in which she can see that.

"Coming from where I did and having to go out in the world and make something from nothing has been a tremendous amount of hard work. But the horses were always there for me. I've been saved by horses and now I'm trying to help save them."

TAMEE ZIMMERMAN

"I was trying to figure out how to work with horses from a relationship standpoint, in a balanced partnership."

The mesa west of the Rio Grande Gorge is no place for agoraphobics. It's wide-open space with a vengeance: a treeless, windswept expanse of sagebrush and rock-studded dirt. The views are, of course, amazing. The Sangre de Cristo Mountains punctuate the eastern skyline on the Taos side of the Gorge; the Pedernales and the Brazos mark the far western horizon, where the setting sun stages psychedelic light shows on summer evenings. If "Don't Fence Me In" is your theme song, you'll feel right at home out here.

Tamee Zimmerman and her husband Ray might have had Cole Porter's lyrics in mind when they left Southern California for Taos in search of a residential antidote to their high-pressure jobs in the film industry. They wanted land, lots of land, with starry, not smoggy, skies above. They also liked the idea of living off-grid and doing their part to conserve the earth's dwindling resources. When they found an energy-self-sufficient contemporary house on forty acres bordering the Rio Grande Gorge they decided it was the perfect place to transplant themselves, their three dogs, and Tamee's three horses.

"Having horses pushed me up into Topanga Canyon when we were in LA," Tamee explains, "and from there to Taos. My whole life has been about getting back to some semblance of the feeling I had being raised in the country. It's a whole different set of problems, living in the country, but it's a way of life that's hard to explain to someone who hasn't experienced it when they were young. They can't understand what it's like to always yearn for it. It's like you have to get back to it and if you don't you're going to die or not be who you're meant to be."

Tamee did grow up in the country starting with a ranch on the Nebraska/Iowa border where her father raised Quarter Horses. She first sat on a horse at age two, and when she was seven her father bought a mustang mare in foal, who produced a filly that became Tamee's first horse, April. April and her father's horses were, in Tamee's words, "lifesavers," providing continuity and stability in a childhood marked by her parents' divorce and subsequent relocations.

"My parents split up when I was eighteen months old. I was always either with my mother or with my father, not with both. My father moved from the Midwest to northern California with his Quarter Horses and April. My mother had health issues. She couldn't handle the humidity in Iowa so we moved quite a few times trying to find the right place for her. We finally settled in LA when I was in the sixth grade.

"I'd spend the summers with my father and I'd see the same horses every year. He had a gorgeous Appaloosa stallion named Chief and another horse, Sugar, who was literally a purple horse, the color of red wine. We would race the quarter mile with these horses and just go flat out. I always rode bareback as a child; my father used to say I was part Indian because I was just glued to the backs of these horses."

But the idyllic summers of riding daily in the hills of Marin County in northern California came to an end when Tamee was in high school.

"My dad sold April without telling me. He had remarried and his new wife wanted Arabians and there was only so much room in the barn. So my horse went by the wayside. I felt horribly betrayed. Later, on his deathbed, my father admitted that he had put his wife's needs ahead of mine. She was only eleven years older than me and this had been her first marriage. I suspect she resented me. Selling my horse may have been a way of ensuring that I didn't come to visit them so much."

This episode of parental betrayal, coupled with a bout of unkind treatment from another family member, probably contributed to Tamee's sensitivity to the inner states of the horses in her life. Even as a young girl, she was critical of conventional training methods based on coercion.

"My father loved and respected horses, but he was an old school trainer. I felt his way was too much about breaking the spirit of the horse. If he couldn't get a horse loaded it was a fight; if a horse was shying at something he'd tie it to a pole so it couldn't get away from the thing that was scaring it. I hated all this so everything I did was the opposite of what he did. I wasn't in a contest with him, but I definitely wanted to show him you don't have to treat horses harshly.

"Even so-called natural horsemanship isn't really natural. It's just non-violent. It rewards by releasing pressure rather than beating your horse to death, but there's no way that's natural. I made up my training as I went along when I was a kid and a teenager. April never had a bit in her mouth; I always rode with a hackamore and she was amazing in it. I have never held a whip in my hand; I have never ridden with a crop or with spurs. I just don't believe in it. I did a lot of work on the ground, just by instinct, without having been taught how important it was. I was trying to figure out how to work with horses from a relationship standpoint, in a balanced partnership instead of from the standpoint of 'I'm going to make you do what I want you to do regardless of whether you want to or not.'"

This desire for a balanced partnership was something Tamee was able to bring to fruition when, as an adult, she got her Arabians, a breed known for their sensitivity, intelligence, and desire to bond with people.

"My father eventually realized that there was no market for cutting horses in northern California so he moved into Arabs and became a show judge and an official of the Arabian Horseman's Association. Once I realized what Arabs give you and what incredible personalities and spirit they have—they are like my standard poodles—I couldn't go back to other breeds.

"I got married when I was forty and that same year I bought my first Arabian horse. My girlfriend had gotten him to show, but he didn't have enough action for her. I wanted to buy him because I practice a way of training that isn't prevalent in the show world and I thought it might suit him better. So Provence, a Spanish Basque Bey, became my project horse. When I first had him he was so skittish you couldn't even lead him down the center aisle of a barn. He would literally go up the walls. I had to work hard at gaining his trust and I had to re-establish my own skills with horses because I had been away from them for years. As a producer in the film business I worked incredibly long hours and was gone a lot and having a horse hadn't been practical."

One of the skills Tamee had to re-establish was her ability to leave the tensions inherent in her professional life at the barn door.

"At first I didn't realize that Provence was picking up on my stress. The last thing I wanted to do was make his stress worse so I started doing meditation before I went to see him. I started clearing myself to be ready to be with him. Actually, having him was the one of the only things that balanced me in the high pressure world of Hollywood."

Once again, as in her childhood, Tamee found refuge in being with a horse, even one as challenging as Provence, whom she describes as being much more like herself than the second Arabian she purchased to keep him company.

"I think I'm more like Provence than Zelly. Zelly is joyful; he's like a dog. I can do anything with him. Provence thinks he's a stallion; he's very much in his horse self. He had a lot of anger and spirit when I got him and yet he needed a lot of nurturing. I think we're alike in many ways."

When she tells me some more about her experiences with Provence, I understand what she means about them both having a strongly independent spirit coupled with a need for emotional support.

"I usually rode out alone when I was a child and if I got into trouble there was no one I could turn to. Also, there was something about getting down and walking home that was completely unacceptable and I knew I would probably get punished for it, just as I would if I brought my horse home overheated or lathered or injured. I had some pretty interesting accidents on horses when I was young, but I always managed to get myself and the horses home without help. As a result I feel like I can cope with just about anything.

"I think the only time I've been stumped was once on Provence when I just couldn't get him to calm down no matter what I did. I know not to get my ego caught up with horses; for me it's all about safety and if you're out there and you can't handle the situation then you shouldn't be out there. But it was really hard to come back from something like what I went through with Provence. I lost my confidence for a while, and that was the first time I ever did, even with all the accidents I'd had earlier. The situation with Provence upset me so much I started riding clinics with Buck Brannaman to really learn horsemanship at a higher level.

"I needed a mentor, someone to say, 'Yes, you had the right idea, but here's how you can expand on it. Or, have you considered this?' And then I would go, 'Oh my God, why didn't I see that? It was right in front of my face.' Buck did that for me. And just watching the way he rides…he's like a god on a horse.

"He actually paid me a compliment in the second clinic I took with him. There were so many horses that he had everyone move to a polo field that had no fencing. This made a lot of the horses jittery and people were losing control right and left, and then the other horses lost it in a domino effect. I was on Provence, who had shaken my confidence so much before, but I was okay. Later Buck told me that I was one of the only people out there whom he wasn't worried about. I never would have asked him to tell me how I did; I would have been utterly mortified to approach him like that. But he offered me this and that's when I regained my confidence."

SANDRA MILLER

"I've had cats and dogs, but there's something about a horse that's like no other animal. There's a synergy, a healing."

In contrast to most of the women I interviewed, Sandy Miller was not a horse crazy little girl. She didn't collect little horse figurines and pester her parents to let her keep a pony in the garage. She grew up in New York City and enjoyed her riding lessons in Central Park and at upstate equestrian centers, but even as a young woman the idea of owning a large time and money-consuming animal never crossed her mind.

"I never wanted a horse. I wanted to be free to travel, to throw a t-shirt in a duffel bag and just go away for the weekend if I felt like it. I didn't want kids, I didn't want to adhere to a schedule, I didn't want to be concerned about anything other than myself. The most responsibility I could handle was cats, which could be left for a few days at a time. I had this standard of being able to feed my cats. That was my only anchor. If I could scrape up thirty-three cents for a can of cat food, I knew my life was okay. If I hadn't had cats I probably would have joined the Peace Corps or worked at a Club Med. I would have done something that was completely anchorless."

So here's Sandy today: she lives in Arroyo Hondo, a village just north of Taos, on a funky seven-acre ranch with her life partner, Mary George Eggborn, aka "Bunny." One of the ranch's many outbuildings houses the studio where Sandy crafts decorative household accessories from slate and metal, and Bunny paints. Various sheds provide shelter for Sandy's livestock: a half-Arab mare, Sheyna; an aging Quarter Horse, Cash; a mini-horse, Princess; two semi-domesticated miniature sheep; a Golden Retriever, Mikey; and two cats. Four boarder horses also reside on the property.

In addition to maintaining this menagerie, Sandy runs a non-profit service organization, Goldstar Animals Helping People. Princess and Mikey are core members of this wholly volunteer-staffed group. Princess is a regular visitor to a local nursing home, where she trots down the corridors to nuzzle the elderly residents and remind them of the agrarian lifestyle that once prevailed in Northern New Mexico. Mikey goes to elementary schools, where he sits beside youngsters with reading problems, calming them with his attentive presence as they sound out the words in the books they've been assigned. (They don't know that Mikey's keen interest in literature is the result of an extensive training program that involved hiding treats between the pages of books.)

So what turned Sandy from a footloose young woman determined to preserve her freedom into a female version of Old MacDonald?

She got a horse. More precisely, she got a corral and decided she needed a horse to fill it. The corral, a ramshackle affair set against the side of a cliff, came with a cabin about ten miles up Taos Canyon. Fleeing Los Angeles in the aftermath of the horrific 1994 Northridge earthquake, she and Bunny sought refuge in New Mexico. The rustic cabin was homey and appealing, as unlike their California home as possible, but the corral was an inspiration. The first thing that came to Sandy's mind when she saw it was, "I could put a horse in there."

"I had this vision of doing my sculpture and craftwork in a workshop with horses in a shed nearby where I could see them. So I immediately leased a horse from Pam MacArthur and then after a couple of months I decided I needed a horse of my own in my daily life. So after only six months in Taos I went to Tucumcari and bought Cash."

Cash was the first in a series of horses that, for one reason or another, weren't keepers. Sandy laughingly describes her history of failed equine relationships as if she were talking about a string of rejected suitors.

"Cash was my first boy. I was in love with him from day one. He was such a gentleman. He would take me out, he would show me a good time, he was very much a well-mannered partner. He wasn't very demonstrative; you had to sit back and let him come to you. He seemed very Taurean. But he was a good date. He was predictable.

"Then I got Bailey as a buddy for him. Cash loved him, but Bailey was totally green and had bad manners. So I got Faro, a big Palomino. Faro turned out to be high strung and buddy sour so that didn't work out either. I also had Bucky, a buckskin gelding, at that time. I have a tendency to get a replacement horse before I sell the old one and then every time I have three horses I run out of money and have to figure out which one to give up.

"Bucky was great; he was another beau. I loved Bucky and I still miss him, but he had navicular disease. Fortunately he ended up with my farrier, who was able to cure him. And Susan Nestor kept Cash off and on to help me out. He's a senior horse and can only be ridden lightly and he needs expensive supplements. Then I got Girlie. She had a nasty attitude so she had to go. I replaced her with Handsome, a big bulky cowboy's horse. He probably would have been fine, but I sent him off to a trainer and he came back like a locomotive. The trainer muscled him up and speeded him up, but he didn't put brakes on him. I couldn't deal with that."

By this time Sandy and Bunny had moved from the canyon cabin to the ranch in Arroyo Hondo, which was nicely set up for livestock.

"The canyon property really wasn't laid out right for horses. But I sometimes get visual images and then go about bringing them into being. This ranch pretty much fell into our hands through friends and we bought it immediately. Now I have a workshop in the old barn and it overlooks a three-acre pasture with a thirty-six foot horse shelter and lots of horses, Sheyna and Cash and my boarders.

"I don't want to pick up and run away for the weekend any more. I want to stay home and have a routine, something I always dreaded years ago. Now I love it. Once I had a horse in my life every day I found stability. I don't have it in myself. On my own I have a lot of chaos and disorganization. But now I'm taking care of six horses, a mini, two sheep, two cats, and a dog. And they all have their needs and I enjoy feeding them and watching them eat and be healthy and satisfied."

Sandy has come a long ways, from being footloose and fancy free to a full-time nurturer, not only of the animals in her care, but also in her public service work with Goldstar. Perhaps it's no coincidence that she's been able to sustain a relationship with her present horse, Sheyna, who promises to be a long-term partner.

"I found Sheyna online. She was the right age, size, and price and she was part Arabian, which I liked, and part Pinto. Our relationship was difficult at first. She'd been a three-day eventer. She was competitive and speedy and jumped everything and she hadn't been ridden for a year before I got her because her owner had been ill. It took me a year to get her to do a nice slow walk, then another year before I trusted her in the mountains. We're on our third year now and she's perfect. She's affectionate and trustworthy and likes hard mountain rides.

"We developed our relationship through time in the saddle and treats, which really worked with her. I gave her some commercial treats for a while; then I found that she had allergies so I stopped giving her treats and she got a little sour. So I found some good treats and she was so happy to have them again that she was willing to do just about anything. I didn't make her work for the treats; I just gave them to her, sometimes when I was on the ground, sometimes in the saddle, sometimes when she got in the trailer. I never imagined how important they would be to her, but they seem to remind her that we're pals.

"I had some fear issues with Sheyna when I first got her. I didn't have to be a good rider with Cash; he was a push button horse. But Sheyna is kind of bouncy and energetic and at first I wanted her to be something other than what she was. Then after a year and a half I decided that this is who she is and I have to adjust to it. Then things got much better. I got over my fear by just riding her and gradually she learned to walk and not to trot unless I ask her to."

Sandy looks around her little animal kingdom, reflecting on the changes in her outer and inner life.

"I've had cats and I've had dogs, but there's something about a horse that's like nothing else, like no other animals. There's a synergy, a healing. Being befriended by a horse is like osmosis. You suck in this magic."

KAREN SOOMEKH

"I'm finally learning that this horse's energy isn't dangerous; it's controllable and it's actually fun."

The first thing Karen Soomekh tells me when I meet her is, "I can ride, but I'm not very brave." We're standing in the arena adjacent to the home she and her late life partner, Ray Kallman, purchased because of its location across from an entrance to the equestrian trail in the Weimer foothills east of Taos.

She mounts one of her five mares and proceeds to circle the arena in textbook form, with a balanced seat, light hands, and precise movements. I can't understand why on earth this woman feels insecure about riding anything, much less one of her well-trained gaited horses.

For that matter, neither can Karen. Some months later, sitting in her living room with a small flock of dogs at our feet (her two Whippets and three Papillons), she tries to make sense of her fear.

"I haven't had a bad horse accident. I haven't had a wreck, or a runaway, or even a bad spook. There isn't anything that my horses have done to scare me. But I've always diligently looked for horses that are very safe and won't challenge me because I'm not up to it."

When Karen tells me about her early experiences with horses and her career as a lawyer specializing in business and insurance litigation, her avowed timidity seems even more implausible.

"I was born with the horse gene. No one else in my family had it. But I was crazy about horses ever since I can remember. I collected those little plastic horses; I counted horses on every trip my family took through the countryside. I have a photo of me at age eight; my parents had stopped the car on a drive and a horse put his head through the fence of his pasture and I had my head against his with this rapturous look on my face. I thought my parents were not at all understanding when they said I couldn't keep a horse in the garage.

"When I was old enough to babysit I saved my money to rent horses and I checked out books from the library to learn how to ride. Then when I was nineteen I got a summer job at a supper club in northern Wisconsin. There was a trail-riding outfit across the road so I would work at night and ride in the daytime. Then I found a stable at home where I leased a horse in the winter. When the lease was up I decided to buy a horse. I was a sophomore in college at the time. So I looked in the paper and saw an ad for what must have been a little Spanish mustang for sale for a hundred and sixty dollars. The ad described him as 'speed in action' and he really was. He could self-collect and canter as slowly as another horse could walk. Shadow was probably fifteen when I bought him and I had him for another fifteen years. My mom learned to ride on him at age fifty, my dad rode him and my three girls learned to ride on him. But when I moved from Wisconsin to Minnesota I left him with my parents since he was so old. They took care of him for the rest of his life and I bought three Arabs for myself and my girls."

Saving babysitting money to rent horses, borrowing books to learn to ride, buying a peppy little horse while in college, Karen, took it upon herself to make her equine dreams a reality. However, somewhere along the way Karen suffered a severe loss of confidence in her horsemanship.

The problem surfaced when another part of her life was disintegrating. A difficult marriage to a man whom she describes as having "a high intensity negative energy that frightened me" came to an end. The divorce was lengthy and acrimonious and the stress infiltrated all parts of Karen's life.

"I went through a time when I became terribly fearful of riding. My favorite Arab had died and I was going through an awful divorce as well as working sixty to eighty hours a week. I was clinically depressed and just struggling to get by. I continued to ride, but for some reason if the horse did so much as take a step sideways I'd panic and have to get off. I became terrified and I sobbed and sobbed. The thing that I loved most I couldn't do. I couldn't ride. For two years or more I didn't ride and I'd barely go out to see the two remaining Arabs. I didn't want to sell them because you're not supposed to make major decisions when you're going through a terrible time."

Fortunately, she met Ray, a gentleman and scholar who was to become her partner for the next ten years. He understood how important horses were to Karen; his developmentally disabled daughter had found great pleasure in them. So Ray, a natural athlete, took up riding at the age of seventy-nine and that inspired Karen to give "the thing she most loved to do" another try.

But despite many positive experiences, her anxiety about unforeseen and unpredictable equestrian disasters persisted. I raised the possibility that the anxiety might be the displaced residue from her traumatic marriage and divorce. When situations are overwhelming and we feel powerless and out of control, fear, like an insidious virus, goes into hiding in our nervous system, only to pop out in seemingly unrelated areas of our lives when something reminds us of the original trauma. And a thousand-pound high-energy horse could certainly remind a woman of the frightening "high intensity energy" of a former spouse.

"Hmm," Karen muses. "I never thought about that. But the timing is suspicious. I sure didn't have this fearfulness when I was younger and bought a horse who lived up to his description as 'speed in action.'"

Regardless of the psychodynamics involved, Karen has found a coping mechanism that works for her. Since she hasn't yet rid herself of her anxiety, she rides only under conditions that won't trigger it. She tells me how she developed this adaptive strategy with Hope, a Rocky Mountain mare she bought a few years ago.

"Hope had a quickness that scared me. I've dumbed all my other horses down so that they have this pokey Quarter Horse walk. When I got Hope I didn't know what to do. I had this lovely new horse and I was scared to ride her. So I asked a friend who is an extremely knowledgeable horsewoman to help me. She rode Beauty, who's twenty-one and just plops along, and I rode Hope behind them. We just plopped along on trail rides until I got used to Hope and could slow her down to the point where she would do a slow trudge when I was on her."

But there were more challenges to come, this time in the form of major losses. And once again Karen's horses provided the emotional support that helped her cope.

"The period of losses started with my mother, who was my best friend and had come to share my love of horses. She was eighty-six and couldn't live with Ray and me in Taos because of the altitude so she moved back to Wisconsin. I took her to Minnesota to see a horse I was interested in buying, a black Fox Trotter. We tried her out and she seemed nice and my mom said, 'I think you should get her and she can be my horse.' And I said, jokingly, 'If it's going to be your horse, you better pay for it,' and she said, quite seriously, 'Do you think they'll take a credit card?'

"So I bought the horse, but since I would be taking her to Taos my mom wouldn't be able to see her again. I had her say goodbye to 'her' horse and after I returned home I'd videotape myself riding the horse and send the tapes to my mother. The next year my mother became very ill and I went back to Wisconsin to be with her until the end. Four days after my mom died, I got a call from Taos and this horse, my mom's horse, was on the operating table with colic. A couple of hours later I got another call, this time from the vet who said her intestine had burst and we'd lost her.

"A few months later we lost a foal to Wobblers' Syndrome. So I bought the sister of Ginger, my first fox trotter. She was only a three-year-old, but nicely gaited and really sweet and she just went into my heart like some of them do. One day I was out feeding the horses and I started to cry, thinking of my mom, her horse that died, and the baby foal that died. Ginger's sister left her food and came over to me and let me hug her and cry on her. Three weeks later this horse was dead too, from a strange undiagnosed neurological disorder. We drove her all the way to the University of Colorado vet school at Fort Collins in an old trailer with no brakes in the middle of the night. They did everything they could, but she just got worse and we had to put her down. This was so painful; that horse had gone into my heart like nothing else.

"After Ray died last year, I thought I'd better get back to riding and not let this emotional issue interfere with me the way the other one did. So I got on Beauty, the steadiest of my horses. She's the one that has healed me. If I'm in a funk or sick or just not feeling up to much, I ride Beauty. That horse totally takes care of me. And then I worked up to Ginger, and finally Hope. Even Hope could not have walked more slowly or more carefully. She sensed that I needed her to look out for me. Now when I get on her she doesn't start out on that fast walk, she just goes plop, plop, plop. I'm finally learning that this horse's energy isn't dangerous, it's controllable and it's actually fun. She's a happy little girl and when I ride her she perks me up."

Saving Horses

Me Sah

Ruth Bourgeois

Margaret Henkels

Bessie Babits

SAVING HORSES

"Beaten horses, starved horses, horses who no longer possess a spirit. They deserve to be loved and respected as much as humanly possible. Let them run free again. Let them no longer be faithful beasts but embrace them as you would a dear friend, for that is what they are."

—Author Unknown

BESSIE BABITS

"Just go ask your horse what he needs...ask and pay attention and listen."

I first met Dr. Bessie Babits on a cold, rainy night under horrible circumstances. My newly purchased three year old gelding, Chance, had suddenly developed a snotty nose, a dangerously high fever, a scary-big lump under his chin and was so weak he could barely move. Quelling my incipient hysteria, I called a local equine specialist, Dr. Douglas Thal, grabbed a blanket from my car, and tried to comfort my miserable baby while we waited for our medical savior. And who shows up? Not the eminent Dr. Thal, but a cute little girl with a long dark braid hanging down her back. It's Dr. Thal's new associate and she looks to be about fourteen years old. I am not reassured. However, my horse, whose judgment is evidently better than mine, is. He willingly accepts her ministrations that night and in the weeks to come and makes a full recovery.

That was back in 2005, and since then Dr. Bessie has ministered to countless Taos horses. She left town for a couple of years, but the great mother mountain called her back, much to the relief of the town's horse people. As we shall see, Bessie had no more choice about where she was going to live than she did about her career. She was born to work with horses and she has never wavered in her pursuit of that goal, and when it came to finding a home, Taos Mountain claimed her as its own.

I manage to squeeze in an interview with Bessie early one morning before she takes off on a full day's worth of farm calls around the county. We meet at a rambling adobe nestled into the fertile ranchland bordering the Rio Pueblo west of town where Bessie lives with her seven horses and a black and white cat left by a previous resident. He weaves between our feet as we make our way to the dining room and settle ourselves in two of the heavy oak chairs surrounding a Mexican colonial style dining table, also left by a previous resident. I position my recorder on the table and Bessie, not a woman ever at a loss for words, tells me how she got from there, Salmon, Idaho, to here.

"I grew up in Idaho, in a little town in a mountain valley near the Montana border. I always knew I was different, even when I was a child. I was a leader, but also a total introvert. I wouldn't socialize with people. I didn't know how to and I didn't want to. I just wanted to be with my horses. I was riding before I was a year old. My great grandfather raised champion Belgian horses and I think I inherited his love of horses and my parents supported it.

"I was a straight-A student and a valedictorian and I loved to learn, but I hated school. I just wanted to ride and train horses. But I knew I needed a good education and I'd worked with local vets and I liked medicine so when I had to decide between vet school and being a horse trainer I got into a pre-vet program at Washington State University. I didn't want to muck around studying other things that I would have promptly forgotten. So I spent two years as an undergrad and then three years in vet school and finished everything in six years.

"I was fascinated with anatomy and physics and biomechanics, with how things work, with the artistry of how everything is put together and how it makes you live and breathe. And I like to fix things. I get such great satisfaction from looking at something that's broken or hurt and making it better. But then a whole other aspect came into my work when I got hit by lightning."

I already know Bessie is not your run-of-the-mill veterinarian—she plays the Native American flute and has recorded a CD or two, she paints, and she breeds magnificent Andalusians—but this statement demands an explanation. I push the recorder closer to her to be sure and capture every word.

"It was around the year 2000. I was still in vet school, but I was at home at the time. My father and I would ride our horses in the mountains when I wasn't working. We were out on some rangeland near Salmon when an enormous thunderstorm came up. I'd always been attracted to lightning because of the intensity of the energy. I'm a kind of intense high-energy person. The lightning was bouncing around and I was on a little knob trying to get down and all of a sudden I felt really strange. I got hot, I felt like I wasn't there, and then there was a flash of white light. My horse went straight up in the air and I came off. Then I woke up. I didn't know what had happened. I remember coming off my horse, then I must have been unconscious for a few moments; then we caught my horse and I got back on.

"That entire summer lightning followed me. I walked into a barn to hook up some Morgan horses I was training to drive and the barn got hit by lightning. I walked into a shed to get some tack and the entire shed was lined with St. Elmo's fire. At the time I knew the lightning business had some sort of meaning and I knew it had done something to me inside. I haven't been able to wear wristwatches since it happened. They inevitably stop.

"But it's only the past two or three years that I've stopped fearing it and started to understand how it changed something within me. I became so much more aware of how animals feel. For example, I would be driving my truck down the road past a horse and the horse would look at me and I would notice and go, 'Hmm, he's telling me something.' I'm more subtly aware of how the spiritual or mental or emotional expressions of an animal or a person are translated through the body. I've always been able to look for a lameness or listen to a heartbeat or see that an animal is depressed, but there is something more now. There's more of a connection with the animals that allows me to better determine what's wrong and how to help them.

"Even though I've had lots of accidents, that connection has helped me be safer in working with horses. I can tell that they know I'm helping them and I'm not a threat. I can come up with a big needle and they'll just stand still. I've done things to horses without drugs or stocks or restraints that should have gotten me hurt, but the horses just stood there. I can't exactly explain just how the lightning strike did this, but it put me on a different wavelength where I became more aware of the spirit within creatures.

"Just recently I was called to see a horse out on the Pueblo. The owner wanted to see if anything could be done or if it was time to put her down. This mare was in a pasture way up by the mountains on the far side of a bog. She had been down for three days. I walked into the pasture and the owner was amazed; she was standing. But she couldn't bear weight on one leg. She had a severe wound that penetrated her distal tendon sheath and was infected. She was skinny and just oozing pain; you could feel it everywhere in her. We were discussing what to do and the owner thought it was her time to go, but she turned around and looked at me and her eyes just burned into my head. I felt inside I could fix her. Modern medicine can fix lots of things if you know how to use it appropriately and you do the work. But finances were a concern so I told the owners that I would donate my time if they would pay for the drugs. Now the mare is sound. The wound is almost entirely healed and every time I go out to change her bandage she walks up to the fence and her expression is so happy. She just feels good.

"Another case was a donkey that had been colicking. He had a lesion and surgery was indicated, but the owners were reluctant to do it. But he was such a neat little donkey—you get a feel from certain animals—and we connected when he looked at me. I talked to the clients and told them that he would die if he weren't put on IV fluids, which was the minimum we could do. Now he's alive and doing well even though he didn't have the surgery. When animals want to be here and it is appropriate for them to be with us they'll stick around—if we let them know that we them want to stay."

Bessie's cell rings intermittently during our interview and she takes the calls to see if there's something that needs her immediate attention. So far the calls have been routine, but I'm concerned about infringing on what little free time she has. I ask her if her demanding and unpredictable work schedule is as exhausting as it appears to be. She shakes her head in an emphatic "no."

"My work has never been draining because I get my energy from the horses. I forfeit sleep and I forfeit food and I go out and work my own horses and they fuel me. What's overwhelming for me is dealing with everyday living. For example, that telephone. I hear that mechanical ring and it's irritating. Computers. The post office. The bank. It's all the human-created things in the environment that I have a hard time dealing with. Going to the airport and flying to a conference is just mind-boggling for me; I almost can't handle it. But going out and fixing a horse with a broken leg is no problem. What's draining to me is the concrete world, the hubbub, the busyness, watching people going about their daily lives not even knowing what they're doing because they're so involved with their computers, their games, Facebook, and all this stuff that doesn't mean anything. It's superfluous and it's all going to disappear. But the horses fuel me one hundred per cent."

This is my cue to ask her about her own horses, six Andalusians and one Quarter Horse.

"The Quarter Horse is Dusty. He's thirty-one and he went to vet school with me. He's saved my life on the trail and in other ways. When I was young I had a lot of pain and digestive problems, and no one knew what caused them. They still don't, but I've learned to deal with it. I remember being so frustrated that I didn't even want to be here. I was very young and I knew I was on the earth for a reason, but at times it was like, why? Because I hated what was going on with me. Then I'd go out and talk to

Dusty, and he'd just stand there and listen. That's what horses do. They listen. But you have to be honest. They won't deal with dishonesty; they'll just walk away from you.

"Beau, my white Spanish horse is especially adept at reading people. If he doesn't like someone he won't have anything to do with them. I've met some questionable individuals in my life and that horse would always place himself between me and those people. Always. Horses console you, they're compassionate, they're loyal, they're really everything. Riso, my big bay stallion, is everything I wish I could find in a person. He's the epitome of perfection and he knows it. We're closer than close. He had a very difficult life, very unfair harsh training. He stood in a stall that wasn't mucked out for a year and yet his mind is all right. I can be in the worst mood and then I gaze at that equine beauty and perfection and I just go, 'Yes!'"

I'm curious about how the enhanced perception that grew out of Bessie's close encounter with the lightning gods affects her relationship with her own horses. She's told me how it made her a better healer; now I'd like to know if it has enhanced her work with the high-powered, hyper-aware Andalusians that she says "have the same energy and sensitivity" that she does.

"The increased sensitivity has really helped my training. I actually can have a hot temper. Usually I'm very patient, but when I'm extremely stressed sometimes my temper flares. I've never taken it out on a horse, but I am very aware of it. So the sensitivity has helped me notice when I'm starting to get frustrated and also when the horse is starting to get frustrated because he doesn't understand what I'm asking him to do. I can see when a horse's misbehavior is due to my pushing him beyond his limits.

"I'm also much quicker to say 'good job, now let's walk and relax,' when I get even a little bit of what I want, say, a brilliant half stride of what I'm asking for. I'm quicker to recognize the appropriate timing of aids, rewards and corrections. Also, since that time of gaining this increased sensitivity and energy I've noticed that the horses I work with have an increased sensitivity and energy too. One of my horses is almost the laziest horse on the planet, but now when I get on him he puffs right up, he's proud. Some of this is due to training and conditioning work, but some of it is in his mind. It's like you and your horse's energies collide. Sometimes that's good and sometimes it's bad. I have certain horses that require me to calm my energy down, to breathe and relax in order to help them lower their energy."

Bessie's words express a theme that has emerged in almost all of these interviews: the necessity to be aware of the interplay of energy between horse and person. All the physical techniques and training aids and trick and equipment in the world pale in comparison to this simple, direct channel of communication.

But the trick is to open this channel. I ask Bessie what she tells horse owners.

"I always tell people something really simple. Just go ask your horse what he needs. All that is required is that you ask and pay attention and listen. That's it."

That's the perfect line with which to end the interview, but I still want to know how the mountain, or some divine intelligence or planning committee, brought Bessie to Taos even though she had no thought of coming here.

"I'm not very good about going with the flow. After I graduated from vet school I went back home to work while I was trying to figure out where to go. I was having this huge angry discussion with myself about how I was going to combine riding and training horses with being a veterinarian. I had a job lined up in California, but the state board exams weren't until April 6, so in the meantime I was training a lot of foundation Quarter Horses for a client in Idaho. On March 7, 2005, I was riding a colt. I had spent lots of time on this colt and we were in a flat pasture without any mud or holes. It was an entirely safe situation. But a little voice in my head said, 'If you put this horse into a lope, he's going to fall.' I answered, 'That's ridiculous,' and I put the horse in a lope and his butt went over his head and I went flying off twenty feet in front of him. He skidded at least ten feet. I landed on my head and my ribs and got a concussion, a fractured skull, a broken nose, broken ribs, and injuries to my spleen and liver. And I wanted to get back on! The owner said I needed to go to the ER, but I drove myself home. Then my father told me to go to the ER, so I did.

"Well, I don't take time off and I don't let pain stop me. Pain doesn't mean anything; it's just a sensation. So I work through it. I tried that for a week and a half until I was riding a skittish filly who spooked really badly and everything inside me tore. I finally had to stop. I was very, very sick and had to go on antibiotics for weeks. I finished them the day I got on the plane to California to take the boards, but I failed the exams by one point. I'd never failed anything in my entire life. So I freaked out. But it was something that needed to happen to teach me humility. Now humility is enormously important to me and I don't ever want to lose it.

"But after that failure I went through some severe anger. I was angry at the world, I was angry at my parents; I didn't know where to go or what to do. I would take off in the morning with a tiny bit of food and run up and down the mountains. I'd get home after dark and I wouldn't talk to anyone. I looked at other jobs, but nothing felt right. Even working my horses didn't feel as good as it should have. Then I came home after a particularly bad day and there was a message from Dr. Thal on my answering machine. I'd visited him in Taos before I got the job in California. And the message said, 'We need an associate.' I called him the next morning and said, 'I'll be there,' and five days later, on July 25, 2005, I was.

"Sometimes it takes an enormous slap upside the head to get us to do what's best for us. There were many signs that I didn't recognize or that I ignored before I got the big one—usually it takes a big one to get my attention—but finally I got it that everything was as it should be. If I had not had the accident I wouldn't be here in Taos. I wouldn't have met Beau, my white Andalusian, or my stallions, or my mares, or bred this gorgeous baby, Olympica. It's funny how you look back and see that you've gone on the proper path. You can also look back and see when you've gone on the wrong one. But sometimes you have to take a detour off your straight-line path before you can get back on it. It's like passing a car in a lane of traffic. And that's what brought me back here the second time. I had to go away and learn a few things about myself and about life and all of a sudden, whoosh. I'm right back where I started. And it's good to be back."

RUTH BOURGEOIS

"People and horses can get past their traumas; it's just part of the process of growth."

R uth and I are sitting in a tiny office tucked into the corner of a big concrete block building housing the Equine Spirit Sanctuary, a non-profit rescue organization that Ruth founded in 2005. The pungent scent of wet chamisa drifts in through the open window and the rumble of receding thunder punctuates our conversation. A brief and violent storm has pelted this stretch of mesa southwest of Taos with much-needed rain and the moist air is like balm to our parched skin. I wonder if the horses standing tails to the wind in the pasture below us are enjoying this respite from July's baking heat as much as we are. I also wonder if Ruth could use a respite from her extensive duties as director of ESS and its associated therapeutic riding program; she looks exhausted. I ask her if she has been working too hard, with all her horse doctoring and training and fund-raising and teaching. She smiles ruefully.

"I once had an astrologer do my chart," she says. "He told me that I was given work to do the minute I hit the ground."

Her non-stop efforts to provide a high standard of care for both her equine charges and her human clients certainly corroborate the astrologer's reading. But it's Ruth's life story that makes me wonder if her destiny was indeed written in the stars.

She grew up in a small town east of Des Moines, Iowa, the only child of parents who had no interest in or experience with horses, but says that she was "born with the horse gene," and had an inexplicable early onset passion for equines.

"I was fascinated by horses from the time I was a baby. I wanted horse statues, not dolls and I always asked for a pony for Christmas, but I never got one. My only experience with horses was the occasional commercial pony ride and seeing a neighbor's horse. But when I was fourteen I got a paper route and saved my money and bought a pony that the neighbors kept for me. I had the pony for several years and my parents never knew I owned him, but they did wonder what happened to the money I earned from my paper route. They had no idea it was going for pasture and feed."

Confused, I ask her how on earth she managed to hide a live pony from her mother and father.

Ruth laughs. She's left out a salient detail: "My parents were both blind. It was pretty easy to hide things from them."

I ask if her parents' visual impairment might be the source of her propensity for caretaking.

"I did feel responsible for them and I sometimes felt I missed out on a lot of things other kids did. But actually I had a pretty good childhood and in retrospect, the things I thought I missed were really not that big a deal."

And they probably weren't that big a deal, given that this horse-crazy little girl had managed, entirely on her own, not only to buy a pony and conceal him from her parents, but also use him as a means of transport for the paper route that paid for his upkeep.

"I boarded the pony, who was a Pinto-Welsh cross, in a pasture about ten blocks from my house and rode my bike back and forth to take care of him. I slung the canvas newspaper bags on either side of him and I had a brick tied to a rope that I carried with me when I rode. When I stopped to get the papers out of the bags to take to the houses I'd just drop the brick down and he was ground-tied.

"That pony was the start of my interest in horse rescue. When I was seventeen I got married and I sold him to people I trusted to take care of him the rest of his life. That didn't happen and I found out later that there had been a really bad ending for him. I felt awful about that. I learned early on that people aren't always truthful when it comes to horses."

The consequences of that youthful marriage were no better for Ruth, but at the time she couldn't conceive of doing what she dreamed of—going to veterinary college. Like Susan Nestor she had limited options.

"It wasn't just that I had parents who were disabled; it was the whole culture. None of my father's family had gone to college. The women got married and had babies. Even though I was a straight-A student I didn't have the opportunity to pursue higher education. So I married my high school boyfriend and left home. Unfortunately, it turned out to be a very abusive marriage and all that sustained me were the two horses I had at the time.

"I stayed in the marriage longer than I should have because of the horses, but when it got really bad we divorced. I became seriously depressed going through the divorce and my doctor counseled me to do something that I truly wanted to do. I told him that the only things that mattered to me were my two horses. So he encouraged me to follow through with that and I went to school and got a degree in horse husbandry."

This wise doctor could not have given Ruth better advice. The degree opened the door to a series of jobs in the equine industry. Ruth worked for trainers, a veterinarian, and at a YMCA children's riding program in Iowa before remarrying and moving to Calgary with her second husband. Needless to say, her two horses accompanied them.

Since Calgary is the epicenter of central Canada's equine world, Ruth found employment easy to come by. She worked at a thoroughbred breeding farm, edited the Alberta Division of the Canadian Thoroughbred Horse Society's newsletter and ultimately obtained a position at Spruce Meadows, the world-renowned show jumping venue. Her professional resume was growing by leaps and bounds.

But the second marriage wasn't. It ended in what Ruth describes as a "midlife crisis situation," and she moved back to Iowa, where she lived for the next sixteen years. Disillusioned with the commercialism of horse businesses, she reoriented her career towards education and outreach programs.

"I got into competitive trail riding and for thirteen years I was the editor of Hoof Print, the North American Trail Ride Conference magazine. I was also commissioner of the Iowan Equestrian Venue, secretary of the Iowa Horse Industry Council and one of the founding members of the Iowa Equestrian Trails Council. I was also a registered lobbyist for horse trails and animal rights issues. My paid work was in publishing, but all my spare time was devoted to serious horse stuff. I did dressage and combined training and schooling shows, I worked with horse rescue organizations in Iowa, I did a lot of work with the kids in Pony Club and sponsored a junior rider in competitive trail. She became the top North American Trail Ride Conference rider in the United States that year. I did all these unpaid things just because I wanted to."

During that period, Ruth created a kind of surrogate family to make up for the end of her second marriage and the loss of her father, who passed on not long after her return to Iowa.

"After my dad died I bought a small acreage near my hometown. I had Jobee, my mare, bred and ended up with Mandy and Dustee, my gelding. Sarah, my eight-year old neighbor, would come over to watch me train Mandy. She told me how much she loved horses so I brought Jobee out of retirement to become her first riding horse. Sarah was like the daughter I never had. Her parents would leave her with me for days at a time. For five years we rode together, we did dressage shows and even a local parade. Of course it wasn't much of a challenge compared to riding Jobee in the Calgary Stampede Parade when I was in Canada!

"After Sarah outgrew Jobee I leased a horse for her to ride and we had a great time until she was about fourteen. At that point I got really sick with fibromyalgia and I couldn't work or provide a horse for Sarah. I had to have Jobee put down because she foundered badly and I gave up all my other horses except for Dustee and Mandy. I tried to persuade Sarah's parents to get her a horse, but they bought her a car instead and she quit coming over. I took it pretty personally; I felt as if they didn't have any use for me and had just viewed me as a free babysitter."

This was a major turning point in Ruth's life, a dark night of the soul that brought her, by a circuitous route, to Taos.

"I was on so many prescription medications it was unbelievable. I was very nearly in a wheel chair with the chronic fatigue, depression and muscle pain. I slept twenty hours a day and only got up in the morning because I had to feed my horses. It's incredible what being in pain 24/7 can do to you; it's just unreal. The horses were my physical and mental therapy. They were the only reason I wanted to live.

"My rheumatologist told me to get used to it because this was as good as it was going to get. Then I woke up one morning and I didn't know what day it was or where I was supposed to be and I thought, 'I can't live the rest of my life like this.' So I quit all the prescription medicines that were screwing me up and started experimenting with every alternative therapy I could get my hands on and using whatever worked.

"Part of my healing journey involved going to a medical intuitive. She told me a lot of things about my past that may or may not have been true, but I listened. She felt that the only place I would be happy in this lifetime was the Southwest and advised me to look at Arizona and New Mexico, where I had supposedly spent many previous lives. So I went to Tucson and Prescott and Sedona. I loved Sedona, but there was no way I could afford to live there. But at that time the NATRC office was in Taos and there was the promise of a job here. So I moved here, and then the job up and left for Colorado. It had been such a horrendous ordeal moving here that there was no way I was going to pack up and go and besides, Taos was at that time a really cool little rural community, about the size of the town I'd come from in Iowa."

Taos also seemed like the ideal place to manifest a lifelong dream of combining a therapeutic riding program with a horse rescue operation.

"It's taken seven years to really get ESS going and I feel like I've put all my life experience together to do this. I've always wanted to work with kids with autism disorders and we have them, and a couple with Down syndrome and some with various learning disabilities. The horse's movement at the walk mimics the way a person walks and it triggers things in the brain that are soothing. It's just magic; suddenly the kids can focus, their behavior problems lessen. And the horses just love the kids. They're extremely tolerant and gentle with them.

"Some of the kids with learning disabilities aren't retarded, but they're totally locked inside themselves because of trauma. We had one kid who couldn't be around anyone. He wouldn't watch the other kids ride. He wouldn't touch a horse. He was just scared to death. We brought out Bindy, our miniature donkey, and had him brush the donkey by himself. The boy came back the next day and got on a horse and by the end of the fall riding sessions he was riding solo, navigating Dustee around the barrels and over the poles in the arena."

Ruth's own horses, Mandy and Dustee, the "family" who came with her from Iowa, are mainstays of the therapeutic riding program, but she also uses some of her rescue horses, a practice that is rarely employed in this country because it's easier to use well-trained senior horses who haven't suffered abuse or neglect.

"These rescued horses need a purpose in life and when you see how they respond to our training and to the kids, whom they just love, you see that they have a life again. They aren't perfect horses, but they're perfect for our program. It's cool to give them a second chance and see what they can do for people."

We sit in silence for a moment. The clouds have dissipated and the late afternoon sun casts a mellow golden light on the red dirt outside the open door. I think about how Ruth's drive to rescue damaged horses and damaged children, to give them a second chance, must have had its origins in her hyper-responsible childhood and the pain of her divorces and illness. As is so often the case, those who have suffered and been healed are moved to become healers themselves. Ruth's concluding statements express the compassion born of painful personal experience.

"We're all disabled in some way, but you should treat people the same regardless of their disabilities. As with horses that have been abused, it's unfortunate that they've suffered, but there's no reason to consider them worthless. People and horses can get past their trauma; it's just part of the process of growth.

"Kat, the little Arab mare we got two years ago, is a good example of how the rescue horses respond to the energy and body work and gentle training we use here. Kat had so many issues that no one wanted her. She didn't know where her feet were, she wasn't safe to ride, she wasn't fun to be around, she was high strung and neurotic and you couldn't keep weight on her because she was so agitated she couldn't stand still. She was the last thing you'd look for in a horse for kids. I took her because I felt sorry for her and I have a thing for little white Arabs. I honestly didn't think she'd amount to anything.

"So I spent a year and a half doing ground work with her and getting rid of her issues, but it was when we used her as a model for our art classes that she really blossomed. Everyone went on about how beautiful she was and how she stood so perfectly to have her picture drawn and what a lovely horse she was. She started changing that very first day. Now she's a very self-confident, beautiful horse, sound as a dollar. We're starting to use her with the disabled people and of all the horses here she's the one we can count on not to step on anyone. She is so careful. She's got a job and she knows she's very special."

Loving care, attention, and patient persistence can work miracles, with horses and with humans. The results may not show up when or as we expect, but somewhere, somehow, there will be benefits. As I pick up my bag to leave, Ruth asks me to turn the recorder on so she can tell me one more thing.

"Two summers ago I was having a difficult time. I'd gotten thrown from a horse and got concussed and banged up pretty badly and I had zero financial support for ESS. I was thinking that things were going nowhere and maybe I should get out of the horse business. Then out of the blue I got an email from Sarah, whom I hadn't heard from in all these years. After her rebellious teens, when she quit doing horse things and got into parties and boys, she ended up going to Iowa State University and is now a vet tech. She had looked me up on the Internet and wanted to know if I was the same Ruth she used to ride with. She told me how much she had enjoyed it and how she missed Dustee, whom she had helped train. She's still in Iowa and she sends me emails and photos of herself and her baby boy. And it's really cool because I thought all those years I spent with her were wasted. I was wrong.

"I cried when I read Sarah's email that day thinking of her, my Sarah, all grown up and still with the beautiful smile that always lifted my heart. Then later that same day I found a check for $5,00 in the mail, a completely unexpected donation from a foundation. So I cried some more. Even though I was still injured from the horse accident I now had money to pay the bills. Those two wonderful happenings had to be a sign. I knew that I could not give up on ESS and my lifelong dream and I didn't. I am blessed to be surrounded by these wonderful animals and to share a bit of the wonder and magic that they provide with our visitors, clients, and volunteers. There is always so much we can learn from horses."

MARGARET HENKELS

"We have to come to horses with conscience and patience and friendship. We have to remember that the horse is not thinking up ways to frustrate us."

My horse looks stoned. His eyes are glazed, his head droops, and his ears are skewed to the sides. A passerby might assume that he was on his last legs, but in fact he's merely profoundly relaxed. Margaret Henkels is working her magic on him.

When the vet does a chiropractic adjustment the next day, he's amazed. He calls his assistant to come watch while he runs his hand along Chance's spine. "Look," he says, "this horse is so soft he's like warm butter." I know that prior to Margaret's treatment, Chance was nothing like butter, warm or otherwise. He was carrying his head high, had a hitch in his left hip and was short strided. He moved the way I do the morning after I've skied too many moguls.

Margaret is a certified practitioner of Equine Natural Movement (ENM), a type of bodywork for horses similar to Hellerwork and Rolfing for humans. It releases adhesions and rigidity in the myofascia, the white connective membrane that sheathes muscles, tendons and bones. Loosening and lengthening the myofascia alleviates the imbalances and tightness that come from injury, overuse, aging and even just normal activity. The result is improved range of motion and better self-carriage.

Margaret's career as an equine body worker proves the truth of the adage "Do what you love, the money will follow." Horses were a lifelong love, but until recently she had always worked to support them rather than the other way around. That work began early on, when she saved her babysitting money to rent horses.

"I was horse crazy as a little girl. I started collecting horses figurines when I was four, but I didn't get near a real horse until I was twelve. We lived in Valley Forge, Pennsylvania near a park and the Devon Horse Show and I was always running down to the barns trying to meet people who had horses to lease or rent.

"It took a lot of babysitting to get enough to rent a horse, but by the time I was fifteen I had saved enough money to lease a horse for a month. I got a hard hat and rode in combat boots and jeans and took lessons and did a lot of trail riding. When I went off to college I actually bought a horse, much to the chagrin of my parents. I was at Washington State University in Pullman, which is south of Spokane and surrounded by farmland. I bought a little Quarter-Morgan for two hundred dollars and boarded her for one hundred dollars a month.

"I didn't fit in with the Western people since I didn't grow up on a ranch and run barrels or do reining, and I didn't fit in with the show people. I didn't really hang out with the horsey crowd at all except for the trail riders. I didn't have expensive gear, but I wasn't proud. I think you take what life dishes out and make something of it."

And that's exactly what Margaret has done.

"I got married when I was twenty-seven. I owned two horses, a Spanish Barb mare and a mustang, a pickup truck and a car. When the marriage broke up I moved to Seattle to rebuild my life. I sold the mustang and leased the mare out and was without horses for almost twelve years. I missed them terribly, but I was working nonstop and didn't have the stability for them."

The mare, Kleka, was eventually returned to Margaret and they, plus a new mustang, now live together on a small ranch southwest of Santa Fe, where Margaret has developed her ENM practice.

"I first got interested in this modality when I had Hellerwork done on myself for chronic pain and stiffness and I realized how an injury in one area can affect many different parts of the body. I've been doing it for five years now and it's become my passion. It's different from energy work or massage. The myofascia is the emotional-spiritual part of the body. It responds only to the hand. You cannot get the same results by using acupuncture or a heating pad; the fascia may spread a bit, but the release won't come."

I ask her to tell me more about how Equine Natural Movement therapy works, because, to be honest, I can't figure out how the subtle strokes and finger pressure she uses bring about the very visible changes I've witnessed in both my own horse and the others I've watched her treat.

"Myofascia is a miracle tissue, the only one that permeates the entire organism and is randomly organized. If the myofascia in one area becomes stiff or glue-like from injury or overuse, range of motion in that area is lost, but more distant parts of the body may also be affected. For example, a horse bangs his poll getting in the trailer and his occipital bone gets misaligned. This affects the whole cranium and the resultant tightness in the skull can spread to the neck and one of the shoulders. Then to compensate for the stiff shoulder, the hindquarter has to work harder. When the hindquarter is affected, the knee may have to compensate. I always look at the knees because horses will try to hide any kind of injury that affects their mobility. They don't want a predator to target them and take them down because they can't keep up with the herd. They are hardwired genetically to compensate for an injury by disguising it. So it takes time to work through the three layers of myofascia to get to the core problem.

"When I go to do this work I clear my mind completely of everything else. The founder of ENM, Joseph Freeman, used to say, 'Never come to this work without one hundred per cent attention. A horse is capable of knocking you across the room.' I forget whatever the owner tells me and just get my hands on the horse and find out what's going on. I do two full passes of a basic stroke pattern on each side and often the horses change after the first pass. Just that little bit of touch can be enough. I work in the mouth, on the gums, the space between the teeth on the lower jaw. I've found that whatever the horses need they accept. If they don't accept it, it's usually because they don't need it or because it's too soon for that kind of contact in that spot. I also look for energy cysts, which I learned about from the work of Doris Halstead and Carrie Cameron. Energy cysts are spots where the energy of a trauma has entered the body and gotten walled off; they hold emotional memories and when the cyst is dissolved through touch the horse may recall the original trauma and react or transform. I'm always prepared for that.

"I had one horse who was very difficult; he was a biter and he couldn't tolerate being groomed because of a history of abuse. Now, after eleven sessions, he never guards his body or fidgets when I work on him and his owner can enjoy him safely. All the body constrictions are released and as the fascia is released, the emotional trauma is released too. When I work on a horse I have to see its eyes. When the eye is in that 'still point,' with the horse looking very focused and intense, that's when I know a release is taking place."

Margaret has quite a bit to say about the expectations that people hold for their horses and how people fail to take into account both the horse's point of view and the effect that their own physical condition has on the horse. She makes a strong case for understanding and empathy and dropping our agendas about our equine partners.

"We have to come to horses with conscience and patience and friendship. We have to remember that the horse is not thinking up ways to frustrate us. They're doing the best they can with what they bring to the table. We forget that they have their histories of injuries, of misuse, and that they have genetic strengths and weakness. We need to take all of this into consideration instead of thinking, 'You're not doing what I want. What's your problem?' Worse yet, we try to fix the so-called problem by getting more equipment, a harsher bit, a longer crop, different shoes to get more lift or to lengthen stride. But length of stride isn't about shoeing or even training. It's about getting the shoulder open so the horse can extend his foreleg. Most horses have the same problems we do: tight ribs, tight shoulders, contracted necks, cranial-sacral issues, and headaches."

And that brings us to the subject of rider fitness. How fair is it to expect maximum physical performance from a horse when we, as riders, may be inadvertently hampering them through our own lack of flexibility and balance?

"Most of us aren't that fit; even young riders have injuries and restrictions. When we're trying to improve a canter or pick up a lead we have to remember to soften the horse and make it fun. And we need to work on our own softening and balancing. How can we ask the horse to do that without doing it ourselves? I've noticed that flexible, fit horses usually have flexible, fit riders. A lot of the horses I work on have older riders and the horses themselves aren't that young. We could do yoga or stretching for half an hour before we ride. When I was having bodywork done on myself, I found that I was so screwed up that when I got on my horse after a session, everything felt different. One leg felt four inches longer than the other. I had always thought my stirrups were uneven, but my legs were the problem. I finally understood what I had been doing to my horse all those years."

Manipulating the myofascia wasn't the only skill Margaret acquired through studying Equine Natural Movement. She also gained a keen ability to communicate with her four-legged clients.

"Joseph Freeman says the way he did it was to look the horse in the eye and mentally ask, 'How are you? Is there anything bothering you?' The horse would shoot him a brief answer; it might come in words, but it would be very brief.

"How it works for me is that instead of going out to the corral and chattering to the horse, I walk out and silently ask the horse, 'How are you feeling? Is there anything you want to tell me?' Sometimes the horse will say he is stiff or he'll look at a spot on himself or touch it with his nose. Some are so surprised that I'm sending a thought that they just look at me and don't say anything. But if you are quiet in your mind and direct a thought to them they will hear.

"My thirty-nine year old mare Kleka is my soul mate and she talks to me. She's not a raving conversationalist, but she does tell me what's going on with her. She told me one day, 'I hate getting old' and I said, 'Well, I do too.' What else can you say? You can't deny the truth. Horses are brutally honest. They like for us to be one hundred per cent honest too. If they choose to talk to me I have to be truthful.

"I had something remarkable happen the other day. I had awakened early and read the paper. There was a story about a terrible barn fire in Ohio that killed a group of broodmares and a stallion. But I put it out of my mind because I had to work on three horses and when I'm on my way to a job I don't ever play the radio or think about politics or much of anything. When I'm with horses I allow my mind to go completely right-brained and fogged and empty of opinions or evaluations. So I started working on the first horse and he was very happy with what I was doing, but at one point he turned his head to me and said, 'I know about the fire.' I was stunned. Tears came to my eyes because he did know. Horses are telepathic and they have genetic memory. Warmbloods were the horses of the knights. They've seen battles, they know about swords, about being wounded, about suffering and dying.

"Another horse in the lineup said to me, 'I don't like my owner.' I didn't ask for this; I don't ask about things like that. My job is to be completely present with what is in the horse's body and with whatever they chose to share and to offer whatever I have that can be helpful to them. So I just responded, 'I understand.' It just wasn't a happy marriage. That happens. Not every horse likes his owner or his barn mate or his barn manager.

"I think many people don't understand that horses have a whole universe of their own. The sun doesn't always rise and set on the owner. I have become profoundly humbled by my experience of this equine world. We're really just guests in their universe. Horses are sentient beings and they don't need our judgments about what their mistakes are or what they can or can't do. They know those things—and they know what we're saying about them. What they want from us more than anything is to feel heard and appreciated for who they are."

ME SAH

"There are a lot of horses that don't feel like they're being heard and they aren't. Horses are willing to be in an equal partnership but they don't like to be dominated."

I first met Me Sah at a workshop she gave at the Equine Spirit Sanctuary. Me Sah and Ruth Bourgeois had been friends in Iowa and both have now made New Mexico their home. Ruth had told me that Me Sah was an experienced horse trainer and animal communicator. I wondered if her training methods would reveal some esoteric communication skills that I could use to improve my conversations with Chance, who has always been a horse with highly developed opinions.

I must have expected Me Sah to resemble one of the overtly assertive, hard-muscled female horse trainers I've met in the past because I was taken aback when I saw a diminutive wisp of a woman with a halo of curly red hair standing quietly in the ESS arena with the workshop participants. I was too far away to hear what she was saying or see what she was doing, but her presence seemed to have a calming effect on both the horses and their owners.

Later, inside the barn, one of these owners brought out a big Thoroughbred mare so Me Sah could demonstrate the art of animal communication. The mare had been intractably barn-sour and nervous on trails for the past year and the owner wanted to know if she might possibly prefer some other activity to riding out.

"Ask her if she likes dressage," the owner requested. Me Sah looked at the mare for a moment without speaking. She nodded to the horse, apparently acknowledging a transmission of information, and turned to the owner. "She says she doesn't know what dressage is."

That seemed a reasonable answer. I was familiar with the mare and her owner and I was aware that this horse had never been exposed to dressage, a fact that Me Sah couldn't have known. After another interchange, in which Me Sah sent the mare visual images of horses performing dressage maneuvers, we were given: a report the mare thought this dressage business looked interesting and she was willing to try it.

Fast-forward several months. I'm watching the mare, who has had a few elementary dressage lessons with a trainer, perform flawlessly and happily in a training level test at a local show. She is nothing like the nervous, jigging creature I'd always attempted to avoid on trail rides, fearing that she would upset my own horse. I decide that I definitely need to interview Me Sah even though she has only a peripheral connection to Taos.

After circumnavigating several cul-de-sacs in her Santa Fe neighborhood, a rabbit warren of one-story townhouses with a confusing numbering system, I eventually end up at her front door. She greets me warmly and escorts me into a comfortable, normal-looking living room. No crystals, incense or new age paraphernalia in sight, just a cushy sofa and chairs, some books, and a small furry dog who's terrified of me. I'm trying to exude good will and harmlessness, but my animal communication skills are clearly inadequate, at least when it comes to this particular animal. Me Sah explains that he's a rescue dog who's suspicious of strangers and exiles him to a bedroom.

We settle ourselves on the sofa and Me Sah tells me how she came to her present line of work, which involves a lot more than communicating with and training horses. She also does spiritual readings, energy work, and various forms of healing. In fact, there are two strands to her story, the equine and the spiritual, and over the years they have woven themselves together. (There's also a musical interlude, which we'll come to below.)

She begins her story with the usual confession of a childhood equine obsession.

"I was a horse-crazy little girl. I started riding American Saddlebreds when I was seven, in Florida where my family lived. Later, when I was an adult, I was living in the Midwest and got involved with Western riding, barrel racing, showing Quarter Horses. Then, because I'd always wanted to jump, I worked with a jumping trainer, and after him with a trainer for the Austrian Olympic team. When he needed an assistant I turned professional. I've worked in pretty much every riding discipline.

"When I became a professional I had to have a different attitude; as a professional you have to be more detached from the horses and you have to produce. It was a great learning experience because it's a difficult business, full of challenges.

"I learned that everything I did when I was on the back of a horse had an effect on that animal. At the time I'm not sure I related that to how the world works in general, but I did learn that every little movement, every thought, every breath means something to the horse. They are so sensitive. It made me more aware of what was going on inside me. If I got on a horse and I was angry or uptight, the horse would immediately mirror that back to me.

"At one place in Iowa where I worked we got a lot of horses off the track and they forced you to learn how to be quiet internally. The horses I had ridden prior to this were Quarter Horses and a lot of times you have to work to get their energy up; they're inclined to be lazy. These ex-race horses were totally different. There was one in particular, a big powerful Thoroughbred. It took me a couple of years to figure out how to get him calmed down. We would gallop the horses on a mile-long track around a cornfield to condition them. When I was on this horse and we were with other horses he would be like, 'Are we racing now? I'm ready!' And I'd be like, 'I'm a goner, he's about to take off.' I had to force myself to take inner control and be very, very still and calm. Then he would respond to me enough that we didn't have a runaway."

After this initial period of training and teaching, Me Sah segued into the entertainment industry.

"I sort of left the horse world, except when I was back home in Iowa where I helped a friend who owned a stable and always needed someone to take over lessons. I lived in LA and Hollywood for quite a while and played in a lot of bands in California and the West and Midwest. I started out as a drummer, which was unusual for a woman at the time and not that well accepted. I experienced a lot of discrimination. Then I tried the piano, but I was the world's worst piano player. So I started singing more, and playing bass. This lasted about twelve years."

At that point the physical injuries she had incurred during her years of active horse training had finally caught up with her.

"I had a lot of horse-related injuries. I had my ear bitten off when I was seven; I broke my foot, broke my leg, my back got bumped up, I've fallen off horses and horses have fallen on me. I had back surgery when I was forty-four and after that I couldn't ride. I couldn't even sit on a horse. I was upset about that for a while, but I got over it and I'm still working with horses by teaching. I love to watch people get understanding. I love to watch horses learn to relate to people.

"But generally when I'm teaching I focus on the rider because if the rider is not correct it will be bothering the horse and you can fix the problem with the way the horse is going by correcting the rider. Of course one of the problems that people often have is fear of bodily injury. There are a lot of things you can do to deal with that and some of what you do depends on where the fear comes from and what it's really about, which might not be the horse. A lot of fear is about being out of control. There's a center in Wickenburg, Arizona that deals with bulimic and anorexic women. These women feel they have no control over anything in their lives except what they put in their mouths. When they are shown that with the right techniques they can have a semblance of control over a huge strong animal like a horse they are empowered. Equine therapy has been quite successful with anorexics.

"Also, if you can learn how to relate to the horse so that the horse understands what you're trying to say—the horse speaks horse language and we speak human language and there's not always a lot of communication—once you learn how to communicate and you understand that the horse is going to listen and be willing to partner with you, you don't have to be afraid of it. I think if you let the horse feel your fear and don't try to hide it, the horse will tend to take care of you. But don't pretend that you aren't afraid if you are. Horses hate incongruity."

The back surgery put an end not only to Me Sah's riding, but also her music career, since she couldn't go on the road without extreme discomfort. More significantly, it brought about a shift towards healing work and the development of her spiritual gifts.

"I went back to school and got my master's in social work. I went into the mental health field, but got discouraged because I felt people weren't getting helped; they were getting drugged. So I started learning all these alternative treatments that were truly beneficial. Actually, I've been on an intense spiritual path since I was a teenager. So it was natural for me to get into the healing field and into doing spiritual readings."

"I studied one thing and another, but the teachings of the Ascended Masters were always the central thread I followed. I had, and still do have, lots of mystical experiences and visions; I'm very right-brained. I also practiced research-based brain integration techniques that enable you to reprogram and change yourself.

"I believe the animal communication was a natural outcome of those practices. I had no idea I could do it. It started with a black Lab I had. He and I were very close. If he wasn't touching me somewhere he'd be whimpering. He could read me very well. So I started using the feedback loops from the brain integration techniques I was studying and I became aware that information could be passed back and forth. The dog just went crazy when he discovered I could do this. He'd wake me up in the middle of the night and wouldn't go back to sleep until I'd get up and come out and sit on the couch with him and he'd go yada, yada, yada, 'what are we going to do today,' 'you moved this object from here to there.' I happen to be clairvoyant, clairaudient, and clairsentient. I see it, hear it, and feel it. The information can come in any form. So I was communicating with the dog in all these modalities.

"So I thought, if I can talk to a dog, I can talk to horses. My first case was a big paint belonging to a woman in Arizona. He had terrible foot problems, a disease that was eating through the hoof. The vet had diagnosed it and wanted to put him down. The owner didn't want that, but she knew if she couldn't get him to stand she would have to do it. When I arrived at her place the horse was lying on the ground, unable to stand at all. I sat down in the hay and poop and put his head in my lap. I asked him, 'Will you stand?' And he said, 'If my family is here,' meaning his human family. The woman was very open to all this so the family assembled and the horse stood up. It was a long process involving a lot of readings and treatment, but the horse got much better.

"At the time I hadn't mastered the healing techniques that I use these days so I wasn't as helpful as I can be now. But I was just higher than a kite and I started putting it out there that I could do this thing. But I found that sometimes people don't want to hear what the horse wants to say. There are a lot of horses that don't feel like they're being heard and they aren't. Horses are willing to be in an equal partnership, but they don't like to be dominated. Most of the time when people get horses they have an agenda and if I could change anything it would be to get people to be open to what their horses want to do. Get off the ego trip about 'I want to do this and I don't want to do that.' Let the horse tell you what he wants and be willing to meet your horse halfway and you'll have a happy horse. If your horse is happy, you'll be happy.

"I'll give you an example of how people don't listen to their horses. I was doing a series of communication sessions for some people who had a Warmblood operation in Scottsdale. They had a mare who was always kicking and biting and in a perpetual bad mood. Their trainer was a dressage person. But when I talked to the mare she told me, 'I hate dressage. I want to jump.' So I passed this on to the owner and she took some lessons and started to jump with the mare and the mare got very happy. She got sweet.

She was doing what she wanted to do. So it was a great success story. Except that the trainer didn't want to jump. She went back to doing dressage with the horse and the horse reverted to being miserable. It's very difficult for a person who's bought a horse to do a particular thing to change, especially if there was a big investment involved. It's like 'I paid thirty thousand dollars for this animal and it's going to run barrels and I don't care if it likes it or not.' This kind of thing drives me nuts.

"Sometimes my work is a lot of fun. I was doing a session at a ranch in Flagstaff with two girls who were preparing for a huge barrel racing competition. While I was talking to their horses, the husband of one of the girls came along. He was a working cowboy and thought this was all just too way out. So I was talking to this horse and I asked him if he liked the other horses on the ranch and he said yes, but he especially liked a mare who happened to be in a nearby corral. So I tell the people what I'm getting and the cowboy is laughing his head off, thinking I'm crazy. We finished the session and I left and a few days later one of the girls called me and says, 'The funniest thing happened. That horse you were talking to got loose and we went to find him and he was over at that pen hanging out with that mare. My husband just threw his hands up in the air.'"

Me Sah doesn't consider her ability to communicate with horses anything extraordinary. She believes everyone is potentially capable of that kind of interchange because each and every one of us is part of the same continuum of energy. Thus the boundaries between all living beings are permeable and our sense of a separate self is an illusion created by our limited perceptual apparatus. If we had a more inclusive neurological structure we would see that everything, animate and inanimate, is just particles in motion, waves of energy.

She tells me she just finished reading Greg Braden's latest book, *The God Code*, and summarizes what it meant to her.

"Every cell in our bodies or in a horse's body is stamped with a code that can be translated into the words 'God eternal in the body.' If a plant or animal has this stamped in every cell and I do too, we can have a conversation. If people would consider that and relate to their horses as the living, sentient, wise, experienced divine beings that they are, just like us, who knows where we could go? All we have to do from that point is listen."

Better Late ...

Trudy Abrams

Susan Washburn

BETTER LATE...

"It's never too late to be a cowgirl."
— Anonymous

TRUDY ABRAMS

"There are a few things I intend to do before I hit one hundred. Becoming an expert horsewoman is at the top of the list."

Trudy Abrams' house, a two-story gray stucco cottage crowned with a steeply pitched blue metal roof, sits in the middle of three acres of generously irrigated pastureland. There are no horses on those lush acres, but there will be once the pastures are fenced and outfitted with a run-in shed and a hay barn, and once Trudy, in her words, "feels competent enough to know if something's wrong with a horse and what to do before calling the vet." At that point, she'll move her Paso Fino mare, Luna, and her mustang companion, Mojo, from Kimberly Swengel-Casara's boarding barn to their new quarters. The life Trudy envisioned for herself in the home she calls "Tumerudi," Swahili for "we have come back," will have become a reality.

That vision was inspired in part by a photograph that Trudy, recently widowed and living alone in Ohio, received from her daughter, who was completing a residency in psychiatric medicine in Albuquerque. During a visit to Taos, the daughter took a picture of Black Angus cattle grazing in a field with Taos Mountain in the background.

"She called it 'Happy Cows," Trudy recalls, as we're sitting in her dining area noshing on blueberry bagels with cream cheese. "I looked at it and saw Mt. Kenya and Kilimanjaro. I put that photo on my kitchen counter in Yellow Springs and said, 'That's where I want to live.' When I decided to move to Taos I told my realtor that I wanted a piece of land with that view and room for horses. When he showed me this property everything clicked. It had the view, the pasture, and soon it will have the horses."

Trudy was reminded of Mt. Kenya and Kilimanjaro when she saw the Taos photo because she spent several intensely memorable years in East Africa, first in the foothills of Uganda's legendary "Mountains of the Moon," where she was posted with the Peace Corps, and later in Kenya where she and her late husband Rich, an American ex-pat, began their life together. Their daughter, Swala, which means "gazelle" in Swahili, was born in Nairobi.

After returning to the States to teach at Antioch College in Yellow Springs, Ohio, Trudy and Rich visited friends in Santa Fe and were promptly enchanted by northern New Mexico. The vistas, the mountains, the clean dry air, all reminded them of their beloved East African highlands.

"Both Rich and I resonated with the landscape and also with the third world aspects of New Mexico, the little villages like Dixon and Chimayo and Truchas. And I enjoy hearing languages other than English spoken every day. I learned Swahili in Kenya and I expect to learn Spanish now that I live here.

"After Rich died I started to think about moving to New Mexico to be near Swala. I knew I didn't want to live in Albuquerque or Santa Fe because no American city could be as interesting as Nairobi had been. And I didn't want to live in anything resembling the suburbs. Taos was ideal. It's big enough to have hardware and grocery stores, but it's still remote enough to have a lifestyle that includes biking and hiking and being outdoors."

Trudy also intended that lifestyle to include horseback riding, even though she had virtually no experience with horses.

"I didn't dare have even a dream of riding when I was young. My parents were immigrants and we lived in a working-class neighborhood in Rochester, New York. But I sensed even back then that I would be good at it if I ever got a chance. I was a complete tomboy. I climbed fences and trees and I often pretended my bicycle was a horse."

This bit of information doesn't surprise me. Trudy has already told me that when she lived in Yellow Springs she was an EMT, paramedic, and firefighter, and had no qualms about scaling ladders with a forty-pound pack on her back. As if all that weren't sufficiently challenging, she went on to take flying lessons after being widowed.

So trying out a new high-risk sport after moving to Taos wasn't much of a stretch. Promptly after completing the construction of her house, she bought a saddle. The next step was meeting Kimberly Swengel-Casara, who brought in Tilly the Wonder Horse and put Trudy on the fast track to becoming a trail rider.

"Kimberly started me out on Tilly, who is one in a million. Kimberly is very good at teaching beginners and Tilly is a perfect schoolmarm so I learned quickly. I was never afraid on her. She was so perfect that she would do the right thing even if I were giving her the wrong cue. She was just too accommodating. Nine months after I started riding, I told Kimberly to find me a horse of my own so I could learn to ride properly. I said I wanted something small, smart and feisty."

Since Trudy is tiny, determinedly intellectual, and unabashedly outspoken, I can't resist telling her that she might as well be describing herself. She nods agreement.

"Smart has always been important to me," she continues. "So is active. I didn't want something that was going to be reluctant to move. I also specified a Paso Fino because I wanted a horse like Tilly. I hadn't known anything about gaited horses, but once I rode Tilly there was no question that was what I wanted. I remember early on when she went into her fast gait, the quarto. I had enough of a seat by then to move with her and I yelled, 'Oh my God!' I felt like the horse and I were one being. I was so connected to her that my muscles were moving in synch with hers. That's when I told Kimberly, 'Get me a Paso!'

"She looked hard to get me what I wanted and finally found Luna down near Albuquerque. She rode her several times and found she was steady even in a thunderstorm. And she had had two babies and was registered. She's a perlino, white with a blonde mane and tail and blue eyes, a really beautiful horse. Kimberly says you could sprinkle glitter in her mane and make her into a 'My Little Pony' or tie a horn on her head and turn her into a unicorn.

"I loved the way she looked, but I was a little concerned about the blue eyes since they're associated with some problems that dark-eyed horses don't have, but I thought, well, when you have kids you take what you get and this is my horse and I'll take her as she is. From the moment I met her I felt she was my horse."

Trudy may have felt that Luna was her horse, but it soon became clear that Luna had her own ideas about who belonged to whom.

"What I found out pretty quickly was that Luna likes to be in charge. She wants to be the lead mare in the herd and that includes our herd of two. I actually like that about her because when I'm with certain kinds of people I'm the lead mare. But Luna doesn't know that and sometimes she pushes me around. She pokes her nose at me, which I thought was charming and friendly. Then Kimberly explained that it was a gesture of dominance and told me to be more assertive. I hadn't been because I was afraid of making Luna feel bad. I hate cruelty of any sort, emotional or physical, and I always promise my animals two things besides love, attention and food. I promise I will never hurt them or put them in cages. Of course you have to confine your animals for safety, but keeping a horse in a stall is the equivalent of keeping it in a cage."

She pauses reflectively and refills our mugs with her favorite white tea.

"I think I'm also less assertive with Luna than I should be because I have a hot temper myself. Today she bit my hand when I ran out of sweets and I smacked her on the nose. It was a reflex, a human thing to do. Horses don't smack each other on the nose, although from the way she backed off it was apparent that she got the message. When I get pissed off I react. I'm at the other end of the continuum from an abused woman. If you hit me, I'll hit back, and kick you in the balls. I don't think about it; I just do it. So I'm usually very careful about my tendency to lose my temper and that, coupled with my lack of knowledge about horse behavior, probably made me hesitant to discipline Luna when I needed to.

"Another thing Kimberly taught me was that horses read your energy. I always say that I'm a scientist and if it doesn't make sense scientifically I can't buy it. But scientists don't know everything and they have been on the wrong track for a lot of years about a lot of things. I've always known that we put out something, whether it's electromagnetic or pheromones or whatever. I've experienced it myself in people-to-people relationships, like when someone acts as sweet as honey and says all the right things, but I have buzzers going off because I'm picking up some kind of energy that's not good. We who are highly socialized have learned to suppress that information, which is unfortunate. But when you deal with horses you have to encourage it. What you say doesn't matter. Horses and dogs don't have a human language. They believe what they receive in terms of emotional energy because that's the language they understand.

"Some people say I seem to be angry a lot. I'm really not angry, but I am anxious a lot, especially if I'm in a situation where I'm afraid something is going to go wrong. And that produces bad energy that can be interpreted as anger. Sometimes I'd get like that with Luna. I'd jump out of my truck having had a bad day and Kimberly would tell me, 'Lower your energy, Trudy. You're really hot.' I had to learn to do that with Mojo, the mustang, too. He came with a lot of emotional and physical damage and sometimes moved away when I approached him. I had to lower my energy by breathing slowly and doing a few 'oms' and then he'd calm down. Learning about energy levels by being around horses has taught me a lot about myself.

"I've learned a lot about Luna too, especially to be sensitive to her being in a bad mood. That keeps me safe because I know when she's going to be unpredictable so I don't get complacent. I'm not as good at picking up her signals as I'd like to be, but I'm getting better. Now I know when she's pissed. She's the kind of horse that acts up if she doesn't get her way. She was being a real pistol today so I looked her in the eye and said, 'You're bigger than I am, but you don't have opposable thumbs or all this equipment I've got. I have a halter on you and it's attached to a rope and I'm holding that rope. So even though you're looking at me and thinking I'm a little pipsqueak, I'm the one in charge, not you. So who's the lead mare anyway?'"

SUSAN WASHBURN

"I was getting grudging compliance through dominance but I wanted willing cooperation. I wanted to be a friendly leader, not a boss."

When I was four years old something, possibly an image in a children's book, perhaps one of the Norse myths involving Valkyries that my mother used to read to me, triggered a powerful archetypal yearning for a horse of my own. The fact that my parents and I lived in a garage apartment in Madison, Wisconsin, didn't dissuade me. Our landlady, who babysat me while my father was in graduate school and my mother worked as an accountant, had an empty guest room. I figured that would do fine for my future steed.

Needless to say, nothing came of my plan. The nearest I got to a horse for the next four years was an occasional pony ride at an amusement park. But that slight contact with horseflesh was so thrilling that even today I can remember the visceral response I had to plodding around a pipe corral atop a weary, bored Shetland pony. A deep epigenetic hunger had been awakened and was finally being satisfied. After each all-too-brief ride, I dreamily recalled the entire sensory experience: the movement of the horse beneath me, the sweet smell of horse sweat and manure, the creaking of saddle leather, and the soft exhalations of horse breath. I fantasized about my next ride, even though I felt sorry for the ponies walking in endless circles, enduring unfeeling children who didn't know or love them. I wanted to steal them all and release them on the prairie where they could run free.

However, I didn't become a horse thief until I was nine, when we were living in Tuscaloosa, Alabama where my father had secured a professorship at the university. I'd had a week of riding lessons at Girl Scout camp and my need for a horse fix was as compelling as that of an addict for his substance of choice. When I spotted a white horse in a farmer's field near our apartment, I knew instantly what I was going to do. After a few friendly visits to the horse, who was pastured alone and probably grateful for attention, I constructed a halter out of clothesline rope, slipped it on him, and mounted from a fence post. The horse was cooperative, responding to my crude aids and homemade headstall, and I was ecstatic. For the next few weeks, unbeknownst to my parents or the horse's owner, I enjoyed regular bareback rides until I took a little friend along to ride with me. She fell off and broke her shoulder, and I was busted.

However, my parents were sufficiently impressed by my initiative that a few years later they bought me a timeshare in a huge, moody Tennessee Walking Horse mare who regularly attacked the girl who owned her. My parents were unaware of the mare's irascibility and I, while cautious, had the fearlessness of ignorant youth, so the mare and I came to an understanding: she would allow me to tack her up and ride because my persistence was greater than her resistance.

After the horseless years of college, graduate school, marriage and motherhood, I resumed riding on anything I could beg, borrow, or rent. While living in Massachusetts I rode woodland trails in the Berkshires and took hunter-jumper classes near my home outside Boston. This experience culminated in a weeklong eventing camp that required me to take ten consecutive jumps of increasing height and complexity on an unwilling school horse. I made it over them all, but my supply of dauntless courage while airborne was depleted, and I decided that trail riding was all the challenge I needed, given my advancing years.

Even though I found riding every bit as exhilarating as I had when I was a teenager, I didn't consider buying a horse until I moved to Taos in 2002. After two years of riding horses borrowed from Susan Nestor and Sandy Miller, I began to seriously consider the possibility of a horse of my own living on my own property—although not in a guest room.

So eight years ago, at an age when prudent equestriennes either take up dressage or switch to golf, I bought my first horse, a partially finished three-year-old gaited gelding of uncertain parentage. It was a spontaneous act of passion that made no sense. Although I had been browsing the sale listings on equine versions of Match.com and fantasizing about the horse of my dreams, I wasn't contemplating commitment, especially not to an adolescent horse who had been gelded late and had persistent delusions of studly grandeur.

However, I fell in love on our first date. It was more of an accidental encounter than a formal outing. I'd gone with a friend to check out a string of gaited horses in Colorado. My friend was a serious buyer; I was a mere looky-loo hoping to catch a free ride on a spare horse. The spare horse that caught my eye was a little buckskin paint that had just been shipped in from Kentucky. He was a tad underweight and covered in bite marks, but he had a nice short back, good bone, and a refined head with a sweet, kind eye. "If I could buy any horse here," a ranch hand whispered to me, "I'd get that one. He's special."

So I hopped on Chico's Last Chance and followed the ranch owner on a demo trail ride designed to show prospective buyers what his horses could do. Chico, as he was called at the time, was calm, attentive, and bold, willing to go up and down the steepest of arroyos and through mucky hoof-sucking ditches. We struck out on our own on a dirt road beside the freeway. Big noisy speeding trucks? No problem. Narrow horse-eating gates? No worries. He walked through them as if they didn't exist. I was impressed with his demeanor, but I told myself sternly, I wasn't ready to buy a horse. So I dismounted, tied Chico to a hitching post outside the barn, stroked his neck and thanked him for the ride. As I turned to walk away, he tried to break free and follow me. That did it. I felt an invisible cord pulling me back to this little horse with the warm brown eyes.

For the next week I thought about him constantly. I kept seeing the bite marks on his flanks and his protruding hipbones. I was concerned that he was being bullied by the bigger, older horses and wasn't getting his share of the communal hay. I recalled the way he never took his eyes off me as I loaded my things into my friend's truck. I was convinced he missed me as much as I missed him. I was in full-on oxytocin overload, bonded beyond redemption. I sent the trader a deposit, arranged boarding with my friend, and within a week brought Chance, as I rechristened my Chico, home.

In my defense, there were extenuating circumstances surrounding this impulse buying. As I was en route to the horse trader's ranch, my then-husband called to tell me our offer on a twelve-acre horse-friendly property in Durango had been accepted. Since our house in Taos was under contract, this was a huge relief. We now had somewhere to live. Moreover, that somewhere could accommodate equines. I took this as a sign that the universe approved of my newfound love object.

In truth, the intended move to Durango had nothing to do with potential horse-keeping. It was a last-ditch attempt to save a marriage that had gone into a death spiral after my husband and I moved to Taos. He was Chinese and had spent his childhood in Shanghai and his adult life on the Upper East Side of Manhattan. The Land of Enchantment failed to enchant him. "I escaped from a third-world country," he complained, "I don't want to retire in another one." He had a valid point and I didn't dispute it. Taos, as I've noted elsewhere, is not for everyone. Some residents claim to have been drawn here by mysterious forces: a directive from the Pleiades, a picture postcard of Taos Mountain falling out of an atlas, a fortuitous convergence of ley lines beneath the town plaza. We simply came for the skiing, and that wasn't enough to sustain my husband.

As it turned out, my marriage failed despite the relocation to Durango. The Taos house fell out of escrow, the real estate market fell out of bed, and I soon found myself back where I started from, in the house we had built in the foothills east of Taos. But now I had a horse in my backyard. A very young horse who, when he recovered from the case of strangles he'd been incubating when I rode him in Colorado, was not a docile youngster, but a teenager with a bad case of oppositional disorder.

Chance wasn't completely impossible, although Karen Soomekh, after watching him do a convincing imitation of a rodeo bronc in her arena, advised me to sell him before he killed me. He more or less did what I asked but, like Sinatra, he did it his way. He circled the round pen on command but kicked and bucked and looked everywhere but at me in the center. He came to me when I called, but reared upon arrival. He stood tied without pulling back but entertained himself by mouthing everything within reach. I once tethered him at the side of an arena while I worked another horse, and he methodically removed all the whips from a wall rack, glancing at me to gauge my reaction every time he dropped another one on the floor. When I shifted him to an adjacent wall, he rearranged a stack of firewood then quickly released the quick release knot and freed himself.

I didn't mind Chance's quirky sense of humor and obsession with manipulating objects. I laughed when he picked up the cavellettis he was supposed to walk over and I loved the way handed me his feed pan over the top of the pipe corral so I could fill it. But one of his habitual behaviors was unsettling and potentially dangerous. While his self-confidence made solo rides a pleasure, group rides were another story. He had twisting, crow-hopping temper tantrums if I didn't allow him to lead; and if anyone passed us at a canter, all hell broke loose.

I tried every natural horsemanship trick I knew to no avail. Then I did some serious self-examination. After taking one of trainer Karen Scholl's psychologically oriented clinics designed specifically for women, I realized that I did not truly believe I had the right to ask my horse to do anything he didn't want to do. This revelation shook me to the core. Beneath my confident, exuberant persona, a deep-seated feeling of unworthiness lurked in a dark corner of my psyche. Basically, I didn't feel entitled to *anything.* My horse sensed this as a lack of conviction and consequently refused to take me seriously.

So I did a little therapy on myself, taking note of this feeling whenever it cropped up, not just with my horse but in many other areas of my life, including my career as a writer and designer and my attitudes toward money. Exposing this insidious conviction of unworthiness to the light of day revealed it as a fiction left over from early childhood.

As a result I became more authentically assertive with Chance. When he misbehaved I disengaged his hindquarters and rode him in small, punishing circles. I forced him to gait far ahead of the other horses when he surged to the front, to show him that I was the one calling the shots. I played the leapfrog game, riding him for brief periods in the center or rear of the group and only moving to the front after he relaxed. I did more groundwork and more round penning and more lunging.

Some aspects of his behavior improved, but we still had power struggles on group rides, and he continued to indulge in small acts of defiance: nipping, crowding, and evading requests. I was getting grudging compliance through dominance but I wanted willing cooperation. I wanted to be a friendly leader, not a boss who manipulated with threats.

Then a friend offered a suggestion that proved invaluable. "This horse is smart," she said, looking at Chance appraisingly after she shook a rope to back him up Parelli-style and he reared and snorted at her. "And I mean waaaay smart. You need to train him like you'd train a dog." Since I'd owned four Weimaraners, who are both way smart and way independent, I knew what she meant. I abandoned the pressure/release system, the whips and ropes, and strongly assertive body language. I started using lavish verbal praise, treats, and ear rubs. Chance responded so well to this positive reinforcement that I introduced a feeding ritual that I use with all of my dogs. When I presented him with his bucket of pellets in the evening, he had to back away, stand quietly, and wait until I invited him to eat—and do all this while I stood outside the pipe corral where I fed him.

This new regime produced a dramatic improvement in his ground manners, but the me-first-or-else attitude on the trail persisted. I needed more help. Providence delivered it to me via an internet link to something called "Friendship Training," a program begun by a Texan named Chuck Mintzlaff, who probably knows more about natural, in-the-wild equine behavior and horse psychology and physiology than anyone on the planet.

When I joined his online community, I knew I'd found my people. Friendship Training doesn't use whips, ropes, or bits, and the first step in the program involves a more refined version of the feeding ritual I'd already instituted with Chance. Chuck's version is based on his understanding of the equine pair bond, the roughly egalitarian buddy relationship that two horses frequently develop. Buddy horses hang out together, groom one another, and share food. Horse nature being what it is, one member of the pair must be a leader and the other a follower. This differential ranking is expressed when the leader requires his buddy to show deference by waiting for an invitation to eat side by side. Chuck utilizes this symbolic interaction as a means of defining the human handler as both a leader and a trusted friend.

This approach builds a human-equine relationship that is positive and affectionate while being unambiguous in terms of rank. Just as buddy horses are BFFs, so are Friendship-trained horses and their owners, who don't need to mimic the dominant behavior of an alpha mare or a band stallion. The relationship is harmonious and mutually respectful; both human and horse are allowed to express their feelings so long as no one gets hurt.

This training protocol is much slower than more coercive methods, but the videos I've seen of Chuck playing with his horses inspire me to stick with it. Imagine telling six horses at liberty to "take your places" and have them all line up in a specific order and wait patiently for permission to eat their grain. Picture riding your horse bareback and bridleless while both of you are completely enveloped in a large flapping plastic tarp.

The crazy horse tricks shown in these videos are impressive, but what really appeals to me is the manner in which the horses respond to Chuck's requests. They are relaxed and playful and clearly enjoy interacting with him; in fact, they often seek his company rather than that of their herd mates. They clearly are BFFs.

So that's what I'm aspiring to with Chance. Yesterday we went for a walk together in the National Forest behind my house, with him off lead, cavorting and bucking and enjoying his freedom on a sunny day. He galloped up the road and into the sagebrush, grazed a bit on bunch grass, then came to me when I called. We returned home side by side, with him matching his gait to mine, stopping when I stopped, backing up when I stepped backward. He's not perfectly obedient and probably never will be, given his rat-pack tendencies, which I don't want to squelch; but our relationship has matured and deepened to an extent I couldn't have imagined a year ago. We're finally becoming partners.

CONCLUSION

HOW TO HAVE A LOVING RELATIONSHIP WITH YOUR HORSE

B ack in the day, 1981 to be precise, I wrote a book that my publisher, Atheneum, titled *Partners: How to Have a Loving Relationship After Women's Liberation*. A dopey title, I thought, but it did convey my intent. I was tired of watching men and women hurling epithets at one another across a subcultural chasm and, as an anthropologist, I wanted to help them appreciate the view from the other side of the abyss. I was convinced that the male-female communication gap could be bridged with empathy, self-knowledge, and an understanding of the perfidious influence of conventional gender roles.

Promptly after completing the book—and in the midst of a publicity tour—I threw caution and all my worldly possessions to the winds, married a glamorous sociopathic entrepreneur, and moved to New Zealand. This ultimately disastrous coupling demonstrated how deluded I was about heterosexual relationships when they were up close and personal. Properly humiliated, I vowed never again to write anything about men, women, and love.

However, when it comes to horses, I have accumulated a bit of, well, horse sense over the years, as have the women who share their life stories in this book. We don't necessarily agree on all the details of training, equitation, and equipment, because we've all ridden different trails to where we are now, but we do stand on common ground when it comes to wanting mutually satisfying relationships with our horses.

In conclusion, there are four points that are so basic to creating positive horse-to-human relationships that we often overlook them in our concerns with technique, equipment, and, above all, control. They could be called "Four Things Your Horse Really Wants You to Know."

STOP HORSE WHISPERING AND START LISTENING

We are all aware, thanks to John Gray, that men speak Martian and women speak Venusian, and bad translation skills lead to hissy fits in the bedroom and sulking in the man cave. The Equus/Homo sapiens communication gap is equally challenging. Horses are not verbal or even particularly vocal. They exchange information via posture, gestures both overt and subtle, and energetic emanations akin to telepathy. Meanwhile, we attempt to send them messages by making noises, waving sticks and ropes, and executing crude bipedal versions of their meaningful movements. Talk about speaking different languages.

To make matters worse, we humans have concentrated more on what we're saying to horses than what they are saying to us. Yes, much has been written about herd dynamics, the inherently hierarchical nature of equine society, prey animal behavior, and the body language that horses use with one another. But even more has been written about how we humans can utilize this knowledge to our ends: in short, to tell the horse what we want him to do and to make damn sure that he does it. From classical horse-training methods through cowboy "breaking" techniques to so-called "natural" horsemanship and "horse-whispering," the emphasis has always been on our communicating our wishes to them. So we "drive from behind," like stallions with their mares, give the "lead mare stare," when a horse challenges our authority, apply "pressure" (read "discomfort/pain") to an undesired behavior, and release it (read "remove discomfort/pain") to reward the desired behavior.

Maybe we should focus less on how to manipulate our horses and more on understanding what they are thinking and feeling. I mean really understanding, not just "reading" the horse's signals in order to protect ourselves or better achieve our goals. We all know that flattened ears mean displeasure and the possibility of a bite, and a switching tail signals irritation (or too many flies), and a lifted leg warns of an impending kick. We learn to translate these behavioral clues in the spirit of self -preservation, to keep ourselves safe from teeth and hooves and being crushed by a thousand pounds of live animal. But it's still all about us.

What if we were more interested in what was going on with our horses, even if it had nothing to do with us? What if we could remember what Margaret Henkels said about horses having a whole world of their own, and our being "guests in their universe"? What if we could remember what Me Sah said about letting the horse tell us what he wants and be willing to meet him halfway? Wouldn't both of us be happier?

DROP YOUR AGENDA

Generally, whether we're aware of it or not, we go out to the barn with an agenda. Maybe we've got a nice trail ride in the mountains lined up with our friends and we want to load up and move out to get to the meeting place on time. Or we want to work on a collected canter in the arena or practice de-spooking when we ride past that scary rock outcropping where imaginary predators lurk. Or perhaps we just want a relaxing amble down the road near home.

There's nothing wrong with any of these objectives and there's nothing inherently wrong with having an agenda. Unless (a) the agenda is unconscious and/or (b) we hang on to it for dear life even when it doesn't fit the circumstances.

Pam Bishop gave us an example of the first contingency. She described being frustrated when her two project horses didn't comply with her requests. In actuality, the horses didn't understand her cues and hadn't mastered the motor skills needed to perform the moves she wanted. Pam's lesson plan was based on the unconscious assumption that her horses understood what she was asking of them. Not until that light bulb went off in her head during a class did she realize that she "had to step up and teach these horses rather than assume they knew things."

Similarly, Pam MacArthur initially had held some unconscious assumptions concerning Divot's daughter, Prima. She expected Prima to have inherited her mother's athleticism and responsiveness; Pam's agenda was to turn the daughter into the high performance horse her mother could have been if she'd had a more stable temperament. Pam was deeply disappointed in her young horse until she realized that "it was unfair of me to expect Prima to be like Divot; she is who she is."

Fortunately Pam had already learned that dropping your agenda and going with the flow works better than trying to force a horse who got up on the wrong side of the stall to execute a flying lead change or a perfect side pass. And it was Prima's exasperating momma, Divot, who had taught Pam this lesson: "You have no control over what your horse is like in the morning when you go out to the corral. You can have a grand prix horse or a raging bronc. The only thing you can do is make that horse be better at the end of the ride and yourself be a better horseperson."

So when you're in the mood for a fast lope and your horse isn't, or vice versa, it might be helpful to recall Jennifer Siegel's self-observation: "I used to be a person with an agenda. Now I've learned to drop the agenda and play with my horses. When I do that our relationship is infinitely better."

PRACTICE EMOTIONAL HONESTY

The saying "horses never lie" has become a cliché. Nevertheless, it's beneficial to remind ourselves that a horse's external demeanor is an accurate expression of his internal state. A horse that looks relaxed, with a dropped head and ears askew, is relaxed; a horse that looks aroused, with a high head, flared nostrils and tensed musculature, is aroused. There is no pretense, no hypocrisy. Prey animals that cluster in herds to ensure their survival can't afford to dissemble; the herd could not function as a collective whole if individuals disguised their instinctive reactions. There would be endless dysfunctional misunderstandings regarding dominance, danger, and the management of critical resources such as food and water. The herd would fall apart.

Because horses are inherently honest, they find being around creatures that are able to express one thing while feeling another uncomfortable and confusing. They can sense emotional incongruence from twenty feet away. Striding across a corral with an air of calm confidence when your internal energy is going at warp speed is not going to fool the horse you intend to catch. Kimberly Swengel-Casara found this out with her first horse, Tilly, who fled when Kimberly approached in a state of internal agitation. The lesson was repeated with the little red Arab who told her in no uncertain terms, "Lady, you're way too prickly for me." Kimberly made a conscious effort to quiet her mind and emotions by slowing her breathing and visualizing her high-intensity energy discharging itself into the ground. Only then were these horses at ease in her presence.

It isn't necessarily negative energy itself that puts a horse off balance. It's the denial and attempt to cover up those "bad" feelings that we wish we didn't have. If we are aware of and acknowledge them, be they anxiety, fear, or depression if, to use self-help language, we "own" them our horses may actually offer us sympathy. Jen Romero noticed that when she was having a bad day and knew it, in the sense of fully experiencing her negativity, then Sassy would approach and allow herself to be hugged. Similarly, when Pam Bishop, tired, cold and pregnant, complained to her mares about their lack of cooperation while she was pitching them hay on a dark winter night, little Reddy Freddy came close and supported Pam as she clambered down from a fence.

Emotional honesty is a do-it-yourself job. No one else can do it for you. As Jenny Lancaster observed, "You can't walk up to a person and say, 'This is a time for you to be honest about what you feel' and have them do it. They have to figure it out for themselves." When we do figure it out, our horses will almost certainly be happier to hang out with us.

LOVE

This, so to speak, is the heart of the matter, the secret of those gifted individuals who are able to engage horses in joyfully cooperative interaction, apparently free of dominance or coercion. Love is the key to truly dancing with horses.

I'm not talking about romantic love or maternal love or even brotherly love. I'm talking about that nonjudgmental all-embracing state of unity with all-and-everything that exists quietly and often unnoticed at the center of our being. When we find our way to that state, we can, as Susan Nestor puts it, connect with the horse's spirit.

But getting to that state means we have to offload both our romantic fantasies about our horses and our disappointment when those fantasies prove illusory. We fall in love with horses much as we fall in love with people: the horse may correspond to our dream horse and have a "glow," like Jen Romero's Sassy; it may evoke an image of what we'd like to be, as when Madizen reminded Christine Morehart of "those fearless women on their big horses" in the dressage arena. Or a horse can bring out our inner rescuer, as Chance, covered in bite marks and seeking human contact, did for me. So we fall in love—until our dream horse challenges us in one way or another, by bucking, nipping, spooking, or revealing aspects of its personality that weren't readily apparent in the exhilaration of our initial infatuation.

At that point we frequently go into reactive mode. We're disappointed in ourselves and the horse, we question our horsemanship skills, we get frustrated and annoyed, and worst of all, just plain scared when our horses disobey, rebel, or otherwise make it clear that we are not in charge of the situation. None of these reactions help us deal effectively or appropriately with whatever "problem" behavior the horse is exhibiting. Rather, they usually lead us to renew our efforts for control by using more force: more round-penning, increasingly severe bits, and bigger sticks. Or we may simply decide we can't solve the problem ourselves and send the horse off to a trainer.

However, if we can remember the three points outlined above—listen to the horse, drop the agenda, be emotionally honest—we may find we *can* solve the problem. We may be able to sidestep ego and move into that part of ourselves that is, by its very nature, unconditionally loving. Call it spirit, soul, divine nature, essential self—it doesn't matter. What is important is that acting from that state feels so effortless and self-evidently right that we know we are expressing our deep and authentic self and flowing with the energy of the universe.

Our horses are able to live in that state. As Christine Morehart put it, they live in two dimensions, the everyday one we share with them and the timeless transcendent one that is the essence of equine. Like Eckhart Tolle, they understand the power of now. When we step into the still center of our true selves, we can meet on common ground and our horses will respond to us as never before. That's when the miracles happen: the horse with trailer issues suddenly stops resisting and puts first one, then two feet inside the scary tin box on wheels, the habitually aloof horse offers an equine kiss, the itchy-twitchy-bitchy mare sighs and lowers her head. That's when we realize what our horses knew all along, that none of us are isolated, discrete individuals separated by empty space and interspecies differences. Rather, we are all part of a continuum of conscious energy, all made of the same right stuff. That's when we begin to have a loving relationship with our horses.

EPILOGUE

"If there is no need for, or deep desire in, sharing each other's company, if there is no mutual joy of intimate conversation, no sense of belonging to, no all-consuming sensation of oneness, no exhilarating wisp of spiritual harmony, no symbiotic melding of hearts and minds, no deep connection of inner selves, no heart-opening of souls, no freely giving simple pleasures in our journey through life together, then I have utterly failed both myself and my horse."

— Chuck Mintzlaff, originator of Friendship Training, June 18, 2013

APPENDIX

SERVICE PROVIDER CONTACT INFORMATION

Bessie Babits, DVM
Medicine Wheel Equine Center, LLC
www.medicinewheelequine.com
Sangre de Reyes, Classical Riding Academy, Breeders of Fine Spanish Horses
www.sangredereyesandalusians.com
P.O. Box 232
San Cristobal, NM 87564
575-779-2466

Ruth Bourgeois
Equine Spirit Sanctuary
www.equinespiritsanctuary.org
13 Los Caballos Road
Ranchos de Taos, NM 87557
575-758-1212

Margaret Henkels
Certified Equine Natural Movement Practitioner
www.equinenm.com
14A Nova Road, Santa Fe, NM 87507
505-501-2290

Jenny Lancaster
Diamond Horseshoe Ranch
1027 Salazar Road
Taos, NM 87571
575-770-0438

Pam MacArthur
MacArthur Quarter Horses
Boarding, Long/Short Haul Transport
362 Espinoza Road
Ranchos de Taos, NM 87557
575-758-8366

Me Sah
Animal communication, spiritual readings, certified Matrix Energetics practitioner
www.mesah.weebly.com
MESAH1250@yahoo.com
928-606-6289

Sandra Miller
www.goldstaranimalshelpingpeople.com
PO Box 525
Arroyo Hondo, NM 87513
575-758-0123

Chuck Mintzlaff
www.friendshiptraining.org
naturalhorse101@aol.com

Christine Morehart
Equine Assisted Therapy at Ranch de la Paz
horsecontinuum@gmail.com
4301 Tims Road
Santa Ynez, CA 93460
805-350-8837

Karen Scholl
Horsemanship for Women
888-238-3447
info@karenscholl.com
www.KarenScholl.com

Kimberly Swengel-Casara
Pretty-Nice Horses
575-770-6959
kschorsegal@gmail.com

Kim Treiber-Thompson
www.kimandthecaballeros.com
kimt@taosnet.com
P. O. Box 2985
Taos, NM 87571
575-758-7840

RECENT RELEASES FROM

CASA DE SNAPDRAGON LLC

Serenity and Beauty: Reflective Moments in Nature
Rita Mosiman
ISBN: 978-1-937240-19-6
Format: Laminated Hardcover
Retail Price: $27.95
Genre: Photography, Nature

As an avid hiker feeling a strong connection to the land and nature's artistry, I decided to create an art book, which will hopefully assuage the gloomy clouds of recent global economic woes. Nature is inspiring, soothing, exciting, and powerful. It helps us to remember that true beauty in life exists in the simplest of things, which reach every soul open to them if only we look, sense, and feel.

Over Exposed
Terri Muuss
ISBN: 978-1-937240-23-3
Format: Trade Paperback and eBook
Retail Price: Paperback: $13.95/eBook: $4.99
Genre: Poetry

In the pages that follow, Muuss brings us close to what we might describe as the secret war, the intimate war, which resides in closed rooms, in seemingly ordinary homes. Yet these poems are written, reader, with such delicacy, such concern for image, for pause, and purpose-for, in fact, beauty. Yes, these poems and prose pieces turn on the beauty of poetry, of what art can accomplish. I bid you open the book. It is a miracle.

One Calamitous Spring: A Novel of Santa Fe
Edward F. Mendez
ISBN: 978-1-937240-35-6
Format: Trade Paperback/eBook
Retail Price: Paperback: $18.00/eBook: $4.99
Genre: Family Life

Theodora Mercedes has deep Santa Fe roots but her focus is on the present and tomorrow, and not on where she looks, but in what she sees. Making a better world, creating a stronger family, and paying attention to the universe that gives her life are where she puts her energies. So far, Theodora Mercedes has been successful, until one fine April morning when she leaves to visit her sister in Albuquerque. The springtime that follows is marked by disaster, murder, kidnapping, unearthed family secrets, new-found loves, and spiritual crises. Theodora Mercedes has only her wits, equable demeanor, and the gift to help her navigate troubled times and skies. Before summer comes, Theodora Mercedes discovers that she hasn't prevailed alone.

Laws & Loves: Real Stories of the Rattlesnake Lawyer
Jonathan Miller
ISBN: 978-1-937240-41-7
Format: Trade Paperback and eBook
Retail Price: Paperback: $14.95/eBook: $4.99
Genre: Autobiography/Humor

Laws & Loves contains the real stories of the Rattlesnake Lawyer. Jonathan Miller is a practicing criminal defense attorney in New Mexico and the author of eight books. These are the chronicles of his early years, how he learned to balance the law with literature, all while looking for love in all the wrong courtrooms. This book is a must for anyone thinking of practicing law or falling in love.

Made in the USA
Lexington, KY
19 December 2014